FOODIE GUIDE TO BRUSSELS

Local Tips for Restaurants, Shops,

Hotels, and Activities

Alison Cornford-Matheson

First Printing, 2015

ISBN 978-0-9949717-1-5

http://CheeseWeb.eu

Contents

WELCOME TO BRUSSELS

In recent years, the world has gradually come to know something locals have known forever: Belgium is a foodie paradise. Everyone knows Belgian beer, Belgian waffles, and Belgian chocolate are the best of the best, but the food scene in this tiny country is so much richer than these three delicacies.

The secret to Belgium's foodie success is adaptability. While other European cuisines have remained steadfast in their traditions (I'm looking at you France and Italy), Belgium has adopted techniques and ingredients from the countless waves of immigrants, visitors, and even invaders, who have crossed her borders. This mingling of cultures and flavours means endless possibilities for creativity in the kitchen.

There's nowhere better to experience this cross-cultural cuisine than Brussels. In the heart of the European capital, there are more expats and immigrants than Belgians. While this can lead to political complications, it only means good things for foodies. Just about every world cuisine is represented, in Brussels, and international grocery stores abound – if you know where to look.

Because here's the other thing you need to know about Belgians: They like to keep their secrets to themselves. Belgians don't boast about how great their food is - they just eat it. So, armed with this guide, you'll learn how to eat like a Belgian **and** how to eat like an expat in Brussels, (which you'll learn can be two very different things.)

But first, a few words about what you will and won't find in this guide.

What you won't find in this guide

This is not an overview of everything to do in Brussels. If you're looking for a list of every restaurant, museum, and cooking shop in Brussels, with star-ratings or long-winded menu descriptions, this guide is not for you. If you want the latest flash-in-the-pan, trendy eatery, you won't find it here, unless it has genuine staying power.

What you'll find inside this foodie guide

I'll show you the foodie secrets only the locals know, as well as the top restaurants that are actually worth your money. You'll learn where in-the-know local foodies eat, shop, and stay, as well as the top Belgian dishes you've just got to try. After living in Brussels for 11 years, I've hand-picked and tested each location, so consider me your virtual "foodie friend in the city." I'll share quirky foodie facts, personal insights, and words of caution, so you can avoid the tourist traps.

As a Foodie Guide reader, you'll also get free access to a number of resources on our website including: a map of locations mentioned, our favourite food blogs for Brussels, sneak-peeks and updates on future guides, and our ebook, The Top 10 Things to Do in Belgium. You'll also have access to every website link indicated in this book by underlined text. Simply sign up at http://cheeseweb.eu/fgb

If you love delicious local food, menus that change with the seasons and availability of fresh, local produce, dining without another tourist in sight, and you want insider tips so you can make the best decisions about how **you** want to spend your time (and caloric intake) in Brussels, read on!

ESSENTIAL BELGIAN FOODS

Before we dive into the diverse international tastes you can find in Brussels, we need to discuss traditional Belgian foods. Like most cuisines in Europe, Belgian cuisine has strong regional influences, with Walloon foods showing strong French tendencies and Flemish favourites taking influences from their Dutch neighbours. However, to say Flemish food is Dutch and Walloon is French is as gross a misrepresentation as saying the cultures are the same. In food, particularly, Belgians take the very best influences from their neighbours and merge them to create something new, unique, and even better than the original.

In this section, I'll describe some of the most common Belgian dishes, you should absolutely try, and I'll tell you where the locals go to eat them in Brussels.

The Big Four

For true foodies, stalking food in Brussels can be as challenging and exciting as stalking game in Africa. Just like going on safari to spot certain animals, there are a few dishes you just can't leave Brussels without eating. These are the foods Belgium is known around the world for... well, mostly.

Belgian Fries

In fact, the food most loved by Belgians; most integral to Belgian society; and subject of the most heated debates about where to get the best version, is often mis-credited to France. This most important of Belgian foods is the humble French fry.

There's still plenty of controversy surrounding which country can lay claim to having invented the French fried potato. But it doesn't really matter who invented it; just know that Belgians perfected it.

Whether you call them fries, chips, *frites* (French), *frieten* (Dutch), or anything else, the Belgian fry is unlike any other you have ever eaten, and frankly, tasting a good version in Belgium will ruin you on fries eaten anywhere else. (Sorry, not sorry.)

The secret to the perfect Belgian fry is two-fold. First, the potato itself must be a soft variety, like the commonly used *Bintje*. But, most importantly, the freshly cut potatoes must be fried twice: First at a lower temperature to cook the inside to a soft, fluffy consistency; and second, quickly at a higher temperature to cook the outside to crispy perfection.

While you can get Belgian fries at virtually any restaurant, they are invariably best from a genuine *friterie* (French) or *frietkot/frituur* (Dutch). These fry shops can be anything from a small building, to a fry truck and the best ones are hotly contested and voted on annually. While most do serve other foods (all of them deep-fried), the emphasis is always on cooking fries to crispy, golden perfection.

Some *friteries* still serve their fries in traditional paper cones, while others have turned to the more convenient but less eco-friendly plastic containers. Either way, any good *frituur* will offer a mind-boggling array of sauces to choose from and, yes, most are mayonnaise based. But, trust me on this one; there really is a sauce for everyone - other than ketchup. Try a*ioli* for a garlicy-mayo hit, or the popular *andalouse*, a mix of mayo and tomato sauce with a hint of paprika. I'm a spicy kind of gal, so my go-to is *samurai sauce*, a kicked-up version of andalouse. If you're brave, you can experiment with anything from peanut to curry sauces, so be Belgian and expand your sauce horizons.

If you ask six Belgians where to get the best frites in Brussels, you'll get six different answers. Chances are, they will all be better than any fries you have eaten elsewhere. Here are a few of my favourites (All of them have won awards for best friterie in Brussels):

Maison Antoine – Place Jourdan, 1040 Etterbeek – There's always a line at this outdoor stand and that's a great sign. You can also take your cone of fries to most of the local bars, as long as you order a drink.

Fritkot – Place de la Chapelle, 1000 Brussels – This fry trailer is close to Grand Place but far enough that you won't find many tourists. Grab a park bench and enjoy.

Friterie St-Josse – Place Saint-Josse, 1210 St-Josse – Although the original owner retired in 2009, the St. Josse institution re-opened and it's almost as good as always. New bonus – friendly service!

Belgian Waffles

As with 'French fries,' there is some confusion about the term 'Belgian waffles.' In fact, there is no one *Belgian* waffle, but rather two types of waffles, both originating in Belgium.

The **Brussels waffle**, or *gaufre de Bruxelles,* is rectangular and flaky. It isn't as sweet as its rival but is often topped with whipped cream, chocolate, ice-cream or various fruit toppings.

The denser **Liège waffle** has rounded edges and crystallised sugar baked into it, making it slightly sticky and sweeter than the Brussels waffle.

You can get both types of waffles from trucks (usually painted yellow) parked around most tourist hot-spots in the city. There is also a surprisingly good chain, called Belgaufre, found in most metro stations around the city centre, adding a tasty smell to the many less pleasant smells of the Belgian underground.

If you want to fancy things up a bit, my favourite Belgian, or rather Liege, waffle comes from the Dandoy Tearoom, steps from the Grand Place. Dandoy is a traditional Belgian cookie maker, with shops around Brussels. (See Gourmet Shops below)

From the street level, the Dandoy shop on Rue Charles Buls looks much like the others. But step inside and you will see a couple of differences. For one, there is normally someone making fresh waffles, behind the counter, to sell as take-away treats. Secondly, you'll notice a set of stairs, heading up to the Tearoom. There, you can sit and enjoy a waffle at your leisure, while admiring the collection of antique speculoos molds decorating the walls.

My favourite Liège waffle comes topped with Belgian cherries, dark chocolate, and vanilla ice-cream - heaven.

Note: Topping either kind of waffle is very un-Belgian, but I never could say no to Belgian dark chocolate.

Also Note: The majority of waffle shops near the Grand Place, like everything in the area, are over-priced and mediocre at best. If you don't want to splurge on a waffle from Dandoy, head to the Belgaufre stand in the Central Station, just a few minutes' walk from Grand Place.

Read this article for more on Dandoy and the best waffles in Brussels.[1]

---

[1] Reminder: underlined text indicates a website link. You can get free access to all of these links at http://cheeseweb.eu/fgb

Belgian Chocolate

If you haven't eaten chocolate **in** Belgium, you probably haven't eaten real Belgian chocolate. Yes, there are a few large Belgian chains, like Leonidas and Godiva, that export chocolates to major international cities, but real Belgian chocolate **must** be eaten fresh. This is because real Belgian *chocolatiers* don't use preservatives, particularly wax, used in most commercial chocolate to make it look shiny.

But second to the actual taste, is the Belgian chocolate buying experience. Walking into a Belgian chocolate shop in Brussels is part of the thrill: the chocolates are carefully stacked by flavour and filling, and the ever-present aroma of chocolate lingers in the air. (Not to mention the availability of the ever-present samples.)

The best thing about Belgian chocolate shops is the ability to hand pick your chocolates and pay for them by weight. If you only want to try one or two, you can, so it's easy (and relatively affordable) to shop around and find your favourite *chocolatier*.

Like fries and waffles, which *chocolatier* is the best in Brussels is subject to debate. I think this matter requires a great deal of personal experimentation, and I've taken my own research very seriously, diligently tasting chocolate after chocolate …

If you have a limited time in the city and want the most chocolate bang for your buck, head to **Grand Sablon**. Grand Sablon (Grote Zavel in Dutch) is a small square (a triangle actually) with the beautiful Notre Dame du Sablon church at its head. It's the heart of the pricey Sablon neighbourhood and you'll see plenty of luxury goods, antiques, and fine-dining restaurants nearby. Grand Sablon also has the highest concentration of chocolate shops, in Brussels.

Here are my top picks:

One of the oldest *chocolatiers* in Sablon, and my personal favourite, is Wittamer. Henri Wittamer began his company in 1910 and it is now run by his son and daughter. Wittamer is the Official Supplier to the Court of Belgium, but we lowly peasants can visit the chocolate shop, bakery, and café on Grand Sablon. My recommendation – climb the stairs to the café on a cold winter's day and warm up with the thickest and best hot chocolate you've ever tasted. Then head over to the chocolate shop for a mixed box of pralines (and for me, an extra bag of raspberry hearts, delish!) **La Maison Wittamer** – 6 - 12-13 Place du Grand Sablon

If Wittamer is classic and traditional, Pierre Marcolini is new and *avant garde*. When you first step into this shop you'd be forgiven for thinking you walked into a jewellery store. The chocolates are displayed in long glass cases, like tiny jewels. The clerks are immaculately dressed in black and handle the chocolates with white gloves. The décor screams decadence, and that is what Marcolini is

16

all about. The cocoa beans are sourced from around the world, as are the unique flavours. Orange blossom, ginger, passion fruit, and mango are just a few of the exotic flavours on offer. **Pierre Marcolini** - Rue des Minimes 1

If you are looking for a truly traditional Belgian praline, look no further than the inventor of this delicacy – Neuhaus. Neuhaus has been making chocolate in Belgium since 1857 and they were my first introduction to real Belgian chocolate. They invented the praline, 'a bite-sized filled chocolate' in 1912 and now their collection includes over 60 flavours, sold in 50 countries around the world.

If you have time, don't miss the original Neuhaus shop in the Galleries Royales (just across from Grand Place), for its pretty Art Nouveau decor. **Neuhaus** - Rue Lebeau 79

My final 'can't miss' *chocolatier* in Sablon is Frederic Blondeel. These luxurious chocolates come beautifully packaged. And, like Wittamer, Blondeel also has a Tearoom, located on the charming Quai aux Briques, off Place Sainte Catherine, in Brussels, where you can sample chocolate delights, including several mind-blowing hot chocolate options. **Frederic Blondeel** - Rue de la Paille 32

The following chocolate shops can also be found on Grand Sablon and are worth a look if you have time:

Many North Americans' first exposure to Belgian chocolate comes in a shiny gold box bearing the name Godiva. Over 75 years ago Joseph Draps founded a chocolate company in Belgium named after Lady Godiva. His son took over and shortened the name to simply Godiva. These days Godiva chocolate can be found from New York to Tokyo or right here in Brussels on the Grand Sablon. **Godiva - Grand Sablon 47/48**

When you're talking about global expansion of a Belgian chocolate company, you can't leave out Leonidas. These little yellow chocolate shops are the 'Golden Arches' of the chocolate world. With 1,400 outlets around the world, chances are you won't have to travel all the way to Belgium for a taste. Nonetheless, you will find an outlet tucked in a corner of Grand Sablon, rounding out the Belgian chocolate offerings on the square. **Leonidas - 41 Place du Grand Sablon**

There is one more Belgian *chocolatier* I just can't fail to mention, even though it's **not** found on Grand Sablon. Zaabär is a relative new-comer on the Belgian chocolate scene and it's pushing the boundaries of flavour. It has beautiful and creative packaging too. Zaabar's red pepper chocolate is one of my all-time favourites and their lavender chocolate is a close second. The shop and factory is well worth a visit if you didn't get your chocolate fill on Grand Sablon. **Zaabär - 125 chaussée de Charleroi**

18

Belgian Beer

If people know only one thing about Belgium, it's Belgium is home to great beer. The beer culture in Belgium is deeply entrenched and the country is home to 6 of the 11 Authentic Trappist Breweries, including one of the World's Best Beers, Westvleteren. From dark Trappist ales to fruity Lambics, there is a Belgian beer for every taste.

The exact number of Belgian beers is contested at anywhere from 500 to 2000. With so many to choose from, it's hard to know where to begin.

In the interest of full disclosure, I'm allergic to beer (a travesty for someone with Belgian dual citizenship). Luckily my husband, Andrew, is a (self-professed) Belgian beer aficionado, who has put as much effort into tasting Belgian beer as I have in tasting chocolate. For this section, I've relied on his extensive writing on Belgian beer.

Belgian beer comes in a variety of flavours, colours, and styles: ales, lagers, pilsners, white, blond, brown, red, abbey, trappist, lambic, gueuze - There is a beer for everyone in Belgium.

The best way to find the beer for you is to visit a great beer bar. In Brussels, you'll find two types of beer bars: those offering phone-book sized menus, bad service, and are notably absent from this book; and those offering a curated selection and passionate staff, eager to share their Belgian beer knowledge.

The best bar in Brussels, to discover beer, is Moeder Lambic Fontainas. Located near the Bourse, it offers 40 beers on tap and a rotating list of 'guest' beer from around Belgium and the world. There is plenty of seating inside and out, making it a good place to meet up with a friend or two. The staff is well versed in beer options and they are happy to make suggestions based on your preferences. Moeder Lambic doesn't serve full meals but they do have excellent cheese and charcuterie plates featuring locally sourced products. **Moeder Lambic Fontainas -** 8 Place Fontainas

Bier Circus comes a close second to Moeder Lambic. With 200 types of beer available, there is something for everyone. The staff is also very helpful and happy to offer suggestions. The food is simple, but homemade and tasty. Each dish features beer as an ingredient. It is a great way to explore beer in a different way. **Bier Circus** - 57 Rue de l'Enseignement

La Porte Noire occupies a red brick cellar, down the hill from Sablon. The bar's entrance is quite imposing, as it is literally a black door behind an iron grate. The bar isn't visible, until you descend the stairs and enter the cellar. La Porte Noire features a dozen beer on tap and 100+ different bottles of beer. They also offer one of the better whiskey selections in the city. The room contains simple benches and tables and sometimes features live music. The staff is very well versed in the beer, however it is often quite busy and noisy, making conversations with the bartender difficult. **La Porte Noire** - 67 Rue des Alexiens

Poechenellekelder is a top tip from a Belgian beer loving friend (who is Belgian himself, so he knows his stuff.) If you make a trip to visit Brussels' most famous statue, the Manneken Pis, you'll find this bar just opposite. The decor is 'eclectic,' including puppets once used in the theatre that used to be in the bar's basement. In fact, the name roughly translates to 'Puppet Cellar.' More importantly, it has a great beer selection and is very (very) Bruxellois - even the bill is written in Brussels dialect. **Poechenellekelder** - Rue du Chêne, 5

If you'd like a few Belgian beers to get you started, the following are Andrew's top picks:

Cantillon, Lambic - Lambic beer is brewed using natural yeasts, found in the air west of Brussels. Removing the need for adding yeasts to break down the sugars, the natural yeast produces a different style of beer unique to Belgium. Typically sour and flat, Lambics are not common on the store shelves. However, take a trip to the Cantillon Brewery, the only Lambic brewery left in Brussels, and try some of their lambics to get a sense of how they age. (See What to Do below)

Girardin, 1882 Fond Gueuze – Gueuze is made by combining lambics of various ages to round out the flavour. It's still sour, but give it a chance. It is a refreshing beverage on a hot day; smooth, and dry, with a hint of fruit. It is a beer I would pair with cheese or seafood. Maybe even moules frites!

Brasserie de la Senne, Zinnebir - Brasserie de la Senne has become a Brussels institution and trying some of their beer is a must. Zinnebir is a blonde beer with a delicious fruity-hop snap. It's great with greasy foods or just on the terrace.

Westmalle Tripel – You can't have a list of favourites without a trappist beer! This blonde is creamy with a touch of citric sourness in the finish. It's best enjoyed on a sunny terrace.

Dochter van de Korenaar, Embrasse - A bit more of a connoisseur beer, this brewery is at the top of my list of beer producers. Embrasse is dark brown, with aromas of chocolate, a touch of vanilla, toasted caramel, and goes down easy. It's a great beer to finish an evening.

Please Don't Call Them 'Belgium'

One way to really make a Belgian (or Belgian food-lover) cringe is to use the word 'Belgium', to describe a food, when you really mean 'Belgian.'

For example: **Don't say** 'Belgium chocolate,' 'Belgium waffles,' or 'Belgium beer,' please. (Please!) Instead be sure to ask for Belgian chocolate, with your Belgian waffle, to be washed down with a Belgian beer (or two).

After all, you wouldn't ask for 'France fries,' you'd ask for 'French fries.' (Of course, once you read this guide, you may ask for 'Belgian fries' too!)

Carbonnade à la Flamande

If I had to pick one favourite Belgian dish, it would be *Carbonnade à la flamande* (French) or *Stoofvlees* (Dutch). This Flemish stew literally translates to 'stew meat' and that's a pretty accurate description.

Carbonnade is beef that is slowly simmered in Belgian beer until it melts in your mouth. The sauce is thickened with a flew slabs of bread slathered in mustard, a bit of onion, and some seasoning. Some chefs add other ingredients like mushrooms or garlic, but the traditional recipe focuses on the beer and beef.

Good Carbonnade is so much more than the sum of its humble parts. In the right hands, Carbonnade can be both rich and slightly tart from the beer. It's the perfect comfort food on a wet winter day, especially as it is invariably served over French fries or mashed potatoes. It warms you from the inside out.

Where to eat it:

- **Café Novo**, a short walk from Grand Place, this café does a great, traditional carbonnade, served with fries. (See the Belgian Classics section for full review). Place de la Vieille Halle aux Blés, 37

- **Willard's Restaurant**, at the Radisson Blu EU hotel, offers a lovely, authentic carbonnade, served with boiled potatoes and apple sauce. (Read my full review of the Radisson EU hotel and restaurant). Rue d´Idalie, 35

Waterzooi

Like Carbonnade, *waterzooi* is a Flemish stew, this time originating in Ghent. Unlike its beefy cousin however, waterzooi is made either with fish or chicken. Waterzooi's sauce is made from vegetable stock, cream, and egg yolks, and it normally contains a variety of vegetables such as leeks, onions, carrots, potatoes, and celeriac.

Waterzooi is a comforting, homey dish and should feel as though your grandma made it (provided your grandma was Flemish and a good cook.) Although some fine-dining restaurants have created upscale versions of this dish, the best places to eat waterzooi, are the checked-tablecloth and chipped china sorts of places that have been cooking waterzooi the same way for generations.

Where to eat it:

- **Les Filles** - The best waterzooi I've had in Brussels was at this family-style restaurant near Place Sainte Catherine. It comes complete with the atmosphere of grandma's house - mismatched china and all. The caveat is Les Filles doesn't have a set menu, so there's no way to guarantee waterzooi will be the option of the day, unless you call ahead. (See Slow Food Restaurants for a full review) 46 vieux Marché aux Grains

- **Bier Circus** - This beer bar has a surprisingly good waterzooi. It's definitely not a romantic first-date kind of restaurant, but if you're after a good waterzooi (outside Ghent) this is it. 57 Rue de l'Enseignement

Vol au Vent

Vol au Vent is Andrew's favourite Belgian food and we've eaten plenty of these creamy chicken dishes over the years. Although we've seen many variations, the traditional Belgian vol au vent is a flaky pastry cup filled with a thick cream sauce and a combination of chicken, mushrooms, and small meatballs. It's another heavy winter dish (but you're probably starting to sense that theme here.)

Where to eat it:

- **T'Cuyperke** - Andrew's favourite vol au vent is not actually **in** Brussels, but it's close enough I felt I needed to mention it. T'Cuyperke is a real family restaurant in Zaventem (near the airport). Everything is made from scratch using excellent ingredients. The service is friendly, multi-lingual, and there won't be a tourist in sight. Stationsstraat 19, Zaventem

- **Les Petits Oignons** - If you can't make your way to Zaventem for vol au vent, this restaurant in Sablon does all of the Belgian classics well. It's on the pricey side but has a nice, modern atmosphere, good food, and pleasant service. Rue de la Régence 25

Grey Shrimp Croquettes

The teeny, tiny North Sea grey shrimp are ubiquitous in Belgium. If you dine at one of the many seafood restaurants in the Sainte Catherine neighbourhood, chances are good you'll be presented with a small bowl of these crunchy crustaceans to snack on. Eating them, shell and all, is a tough thing for many North Americans to wrap their heads around and shelling these tiny shrimps hardly seems worth the effort. But whether you make the mental effort to eat the shell, or the physical effort to peel them, it's worth it to savour the juicy sweetness.

Not only are grey shrimps sweet and delicate, they are part of Belgium's cultural heritage. Traditionally, these shrimps were harvested along the coast, from France to the Netherlands, by fishermen on horseback. The only place this tradition is still practised is the village of Oostduinkerke, on the Belgian coast, and it was recently inscribed on the UNESCO list of Intangible Cultural Heritage of Humanity. If you have the opportunity to see this spectacle you definitely should. (For more information <u>read my article on Belgium's shrimp fishermen on horseback</u>.)

To avoid both peeling and shell crunching, my favourite way to eat grey shrimps is in a **shrimp croquette** (*garnaalkroket,* in Flemish). While there are plenty of bland, frozen, and refried versions served around the city, croquettes made from scratch are a revelation. The outside should be a thin, delicately crispy crust. When you break through, the creamy shrimp mixture should be molten and oozing. They make a perfect starter or snack.

Where to eat it:

- **Noordzee / Mer du Nord** - For a truly local experience, order your croquettes (and a glass of white wine) from this fish counter on Place Sainte Catherine. They're my favourite croquettes in Brussels. Rue Sainte Catherine 45 (See Cheap Eats below)

- **Les Petits Oignons** - If you prefer to try your croquette sitting down, this restaurant is a close runner-up for the best shrimp croquettes in town. Rue de la Régence 25 (See the Belgian Classics below)

Mussels

Moules-frites, (*Mosselen-Friet*, in Flemish) or mussels with fries, is another ubiquitous Belgian dish you can find at just about any café in town. But, like most things, not all mussels are created equal.

The most common way mussels are served in Brussels is steamed in white wine, in big black mussel pots. In addition to wine, *Moules marinières* also contain shallots, parsley, and butter. Other cooking methods include cream, beer, or even mustard sauce.

Mussels, on their own, can be served as an appetizer, especially shared among friends, or you can enjoy them with fries as a main course.

Where to eat it:

- **La Bonne Humeur** - This unassuming looking restaurant has been serving mussels to Bruxellois since 1954, so they know their stuff. They also offer a variety of styles, in addition to the traditional *Moules marinières,* including cream, garlic, green pepper, and even curry. (Read a full review of La Bonne Humeur) Chaussée de Louvain 244

Meatballs

Meatballs are a Belgian favourite, on both sides of the language divide, and are usually a mixture of beef and pork. In Flanders, *balletjes* are often served smothered in tomato sauce, or, sometimes, Frikadellen-style; fried in butter with Belgian cherry sauce.

South of Brussels, *boulets Liégeois* are the rage. These meatballs are served with a rich sauce of beef stock, spices, and *sirop de Liege*, fruit syrup a bit like molasses, made from apples and pears.

Whichever style you prefer, you can guarantee they will come with crispy Belgian frites.

Where to eat it:

- **Balls & Glory** - While not exactly served in the traditional style, I guarantee these will be the best meatballs you've ever eaten. Using locally sourced, mostly organic ingredients, Balls & Glory serves up giant meatballs filled with a variety of sauces. The balls are mainly pork, but there are beef, lamb, chicken and even veggie versions available. Your ball comes served on stoemp (see below) or with a salad. Try the blue cheese or truffle varieties, or stick to the 'retro-balls,' the way grandma made 'em. Lakensestraat 171

Filet Américain

If there's one Belgian dish that takes unassuming North American tourists by surprise, it's *filet américain*. An American fillet? That must be a fancy name for a hamburger right? I'd be lying if I told you Belgians don't laugh a little inside when they watch tourists' facial expressions as they are served a plate of raw beef.

As a Canadian (first) I get it. We're taught from birth to cook meat to death, to save us from bacteria and germs. And rightly so, if you look at our industrialized food chain. It's a case of salmonella waiting to happen.

This isn't quite the case in Europe, where many good restaurants still get their meat direct from a local farmer, or at least from a butcher who does. I'm not going to recommend you walk into any restaurant and tuck into a plate of raw meat. But prepared properly, *filet américain* is perfectly safe to eat and delicious - if you can get beyond your own mental roadblocks about eating raw meat.

So how should your *américain* be prepared? First of all, it should be assembled (sometimes even chopped) in front of you. It also should not be ground meat, but rather, freshly chopped steak. The meat is mixed with onions, spices, and raw egg (in for a penny…). There are often other additions like capers and Worcestershire sauce. Every good restaurant will have its own special recipe.

One other little note of caution: These days, *filet américain* is almost always finely chopped beef. However, traditionally, Belgians ate a lot of horse meat and used it interchangeably with beef, including in *filet américain*. You can still buy horse meat in Belgian grocery stores and you will occasionally find it on traditional restaurant menus. If you aren't comfortable eating Mr. Ed, double check your steak (of any kind) before ordering.

Where to eat it:

- **La Brasserie de Jaloa** - This Brasserie of the popular fine-dining Restaurant Jaloa does many traditional Belgian dishes very well, including *américain*. It's prepared at your table and uses only the freshest ingredients. Place Sainte-Catherine, 5/7 (See Belgian Classics below)

Witloof

Love it or hate it, if you visit Belgium in the colder months, someone will likely serve you *witloof*. Belgian endive, or *chicon* in French, is often served as a side dish, cooked to an unappetizingly mushy consistency. It seems like an afterthought on the plate.

However, Belgian endive can be delightful. The peppery leaves act as a crunchy vehicle for dips or give a snap to salads. Witloof is also great wrapped in pancetta and/or baked into a gratin with cheese. (What isn't?)

As endive rarely features as a main course on menus, it's impossible to offer restaurant suggestions for where to eat the best witloof. If you are dying to try this Belgian staple, visit during the winter months and eat at **any** good Belgian restaurant. Rest assured, endive will turn up somewhere on your plate.

Stoemp

Stoemp is a dish I first encountered in the Netherlands (where it's called *Stamppot*) and my Dutch friends lovingly referred to it as 'war food.' While a dish that is basically potatoes mashed with another vegetable may not sound like haute cuisine, Stoemp can be comforting and delicious when executed by the right hands.

Common combinations include potatoes with carrots, turnip, leeks, spinach, cabbage, or kale. Great stoemp will also include such ingredients as shallots, fresh herbs, spices, and cream.

Where to eat it:

Like witloof, stoemp is an accompaniment rather than the main dish, so it's difficult to recommend a place to try it. **Balls & Glory** offers a stoemp of the day with their meatballs and it often pops up at **Les Filles**.

Boudin

Boudin is a sausage, normally made from pork, or occasionally chicken or veal. Other ingredients vary but can include bread, herbs, spices, onions, and even apples and nuts. It is typical to Belgium and France, but Germany, French Canada, and the Cajuns of the southern United States all have their own versions.

Boudin, in Belgium, comes in two main varieties: *boudin blanc* (white boudin) and *boudin noir* (black boudin). Boudin noir (or *bloedworst,* in Flemish) gets its dark red, almost black, colour from the addition of blood. Boudin blanc is very pale in colour, as there is no blood added, and the mixture often contains milk.

I'll be the first to admit, neither of these combinations sound particularly appetising. But the addition of herbs, spices, and other ingredients, by a true boudin master, can elevate these unappealing looking sausages to new heights.

One of our favourite varieties is the *boudin de Liège*, named after the Walloon city. This is a type of boudin blanc, with the addition of fresh herbs and milk – delicious.

Boudin isn't typically something you'll find in restaurants, but rather, more of a Belgian street food. You can find it at market stalls and food-trucks, typically served in crusty rolls with a variety of toppings, much as we would eat hot dogs.

Flavoured boudin are prevalent around Christmas time and my local market would have varieties of *boudin blanc* containing everything from hazelnuts, to dried apricots, to truffles.

Belgian Cheeses

Unlike their neighbours to the north and south, Belgian cheeses aren't well known. This is a pity. Although there aren't as many varieties as in France, Belgium does produce some unique dairy products well worth seeking out. (And, as the author of a website called CheeseWeb, I'd be remiss if I didn't mention a few of them.)

Belgian Cheeses to try:

- **Trappist & abbey cheeses** - While the Trappist monks are renowned for their beer brewing skills, they also make excellent cheese. Several of them are even designated by the 'Authentic Trappist label', including: **Orval, Westmalle**, and **Chimay**. Top Trappist beer abbey **Westvleteren** also makes several great cheeses, but they don't fall under the 'Authentic Trappist' designation. Other well-known beer making abbeys, such as **Maredsous**, also make great Belgian cheeses.

- **Brussels cheese** - For something truly Bruxellois, watch out for this smooth, spreadable cheese. Don't let the texture fool you though; this is a strong cheese, with a bite!

- **Herve** - Probably the most (in)famous cheese, in Belgium, you can smell Herve, long before you see it coming. This little orange cube smells like ancient gym-socks, but tastes mildly rich and creamy. It is commonly served on bread, with a dollop of Sirop de Liege, making it a pleasant after diner treat.

Where to eat it:

- **Moeder Lambic** - This beer bar offers the best local cheese platter I know of. In fact, it's one of the few places in

Brussels that even offers Belgian cheeses. While many of the fancier restaurants flaunt excellent cheese boards, they are decidedly lacking in Belgian options.

- **La crèmerie de Linkebeek** - The best way to get your hands on local cheeses is to head to a cheese shop and this one on Place Sainte Catherine is excellent. If you are serious about dairy products, this is your store. Rue du Vieux Marché aux Grains 4

- **Le Fraysse** – With more than 65 different cheeses, the benefit here is knowledge. The owners of this organic shop know everything about the origin of their products. (For more info see Gourmet Shops below) Chaussée de Louvain 896, 1140 Evere

Speculoos

Speculoos are hard, flat, spiced cookies, often served with hot drinks and are great for dunking. They are a bit like a ginger-snap, containing flavours of cinnamon, nutmeg, ginger, cloves, cardamom and white pepper.

Speculoos are eaten year-round, but are particularly popular at Christmastime, when bakers make giant St. Nickolas shaped cookies.

NOTE: You may also see this written as speculaas, which is the Dutch term. Speculoos is the Flemish version.

Where to eat it:

- You can find Speculoos just about anywhere, with the individually wrapped Lotus brand being the popular choice of cafés everywhere. However, if you want the real thing, you must try the Speculoos from **Maison Dandoy**, biscuit-makers since 1829. Their speculoos are the perfect mix of soft and crispy, with a distinct spicy taste. Locations around Brussels (See Gourmet Shops Below)

Jenever

Jenever (pronounced Ya-nay-ver) is a Dutch gin, featuring juniper berries. It's an AOC designation that can only legally be produced in Belgium and the Netherlands, as well as two northern French provinces and two German states. *Jenever* is a neutral alcohol, like vodka, that can be flavoured with an endless variety of spices, herbs, fruit, and other flavours.

Traditional jenever comes in *Oude* (Old) and *Jonge* (Young), a designation that has little to do with age, but rather the distilling techniques used. *Oude jenever* is typically smoother and can take on malty qualities like whiskey. While *Oude* and *Jonge* jenever can be an acquired taste, there are a variety of flavoured versions that are much easier to drink. Flavours range from lemon and vanilla to speculoos and even Belgian chocolate.

Where to drink it:

- Like most alcohol, you can purchase jenever at any grocery store. However, the better quality and rarer varieties are more likely found at exclusive liquor stores. The traditional brown pottery bottles of jenever make unique gifts.

- Jenever tends to be more popular in Flanders than in Brussels itself, although most bars will stock at least one *Oude* and one *Jonge* variety. For a bar that specializes in beer and jenever, head to **café Bizon**, which also features live music - a rarity in Brussels. 7 Rue Pont de la Carpe

BRUSSELS' BEST RESTAURANTS

The bulk of this guide is given to restaurants, the heart and soul of the Brussels food scene. As stated in the introduction, this guide includes only the very best I've tried; those I feel represent the city's highest quality.

I've organized the restaurants into loose categories, but many of them fall under multiple headings, so be sure to read through the entire guide.

I've done my utmost to include the most recent information, but the Brussels food scene is constantly on the move. While writing this book, I discovered a few of my favourite restaurants had unfortunately closed. It's possible, by the time this book reaches your hands, others could have joined them. (If you find a change of address or restaurant closure, please don't hesitate to email me, to let me know.)

Likewise, there are constantly new restaurants opening. As I can't possibly test them all, I've recruited some of Brussels top food bloggers to contribute their favourites. You'll find them at the end of the section and they include restaurants of all styles and cuisines.

A Note on Restaurant Websites in Belgium

Throughout this guide, I've also done my best to provide the websites for the restaurants and activities listed. However, as with all things online, these websites are subject to change at a moment's notice. (If you do find a broken link, please don't hesitate to <u>email</u> <u>me</u>, to let me know).

The quality and usefulness of restaurant (and indeed all) websites in Belgium varies dramatically. While some local businesses understand the importance of a web presence and the power of social media, others seem to have only the vaguest concept of the online world. Some restaurants still have no website at all, while others have a page that was created in 2001, complete with blinking text and auto-play music. I recommend turning off your speakers if you peruse any of the websites listed in this guide (except for CheeseWeb.eu - I promise no music will blast from my website). You've been warned.

The (Michelin) Stars

Unless you are made of money (which I'm not) and do nothing but eat in restaurants (which I can, unfortunately, not do), it's almost impossible to keep up with the Michelin starred restaurants in Belgium. In fact, there are more stars in this tiny country, per capita, than anywhere in the world. And while those stars are scattered around the country, a fair number are located in Brussels itself.

At the time of writing there are no remaining three-star Michelins, in Brussels. Four of the city's restaurants have earned two stars.

- Sea Grill

- Comme Chez Soi
- Bon-Bon
- Le Chalet de la Forêt

If you can secure reservations at any of these, and you enjoy Michelin-style dining, they are well worth the financial splurge. I've had the pleasure of eating at all of them, over the years, except Le Chalet. However, I have enjoyed dishes prepared by their chefs at several of Brussels' food festivals. Particularly if you are on a budget, this is a great way to sample dishes from these exclusive restaurants at a fraction of the cost. (See the Food Festival section below.)

Currently, there are 20 one-star Michelin restaurants in Brussels, but these seem to vary widely from one year to the next. You can view the current list on the Michelin website.

As with the rest of this book, in this section, I have only listed the restaurants I have personally tried and recommend. Some retain their stars now, and others no longer hold them, but are still worth visiting.

*Sea Grill ***

Sea Grill is a Brussels institution and has held fast to two Michelin stars, since 1997. If you love seafood, the chance to eat Yves Mattagne's perfectly composed menu of underwater delights is an unforgettable experience.

The décor of the contemporary dining room is comfortable and beautiful, without feeling too stiff and formal. There is also plenty of space between tables, so you never feel crowded. Despite the two-star status, the service is refreshingly friendly, while remaining perfectly professional.

The plating is beautiful, without feeling forced, and the portions are generous by haute-cuisine standards. Mattagne's dishes highlight fresh, local seafood, in modern and creative ways, without ever taking the emphasis away from the star of the show - the delicate seafood flavours.

The highlight of the modern seafood menu, however, is something very traditional indeed. Sea Grill is home to one of only five

Christofle lobster presses in the world; it's the only one in Belgium. The concept of the press, (similar to the duck press) is quite simple. The shell, legs, and head of the lobster are placed inside the 40-kilo silver press. The wheel is then turned to lower the press, squishing out all of the lobster-y juices. The juice is then heated, table-side, into the richest, most incredible lobster bisque imaginable. Finally, the tail and claw meat are added to the bisque and it is served with a side of sautéed rice. It is a lobster-flavoured explosion.

For a truly once-in-a-lifetime seafood experience, Sea Grill is the perfect choice. <u>Sea Grill</u> - Rue Fosse aux Loups 47 (Read my <u>extended review of Sea Grill</u>.)

Bon Bon **

For a two-star Michelin experience, with a more varied menu, **Restaurant Bon Bon** is another excellent choice. You can order dishes a la carte, or choose from a five or seven course set menu. I opted for the five-course *Menu Impro* with accompanying wines.

Bon Bon is located in a large white house, in a green and residential part of Woluwe-Saint-Pierre, far from the bustling city centre. It is particularly pleasant on a warm summer evening, as you can enjoy your *apéro* in the garden terrace.

The restaurant works with 95% bio-organic produce and you can often see the chef nip out to the little *potager* (kitchen garden) to pick herbs for his dishes.

A few stand-outs from my meal were:

- *Les Bijoux d'Huitres "Perle Blance" Menthe corse et gelée de vodka-tonic (*Jewels of 'White Pearl' oysters with Corsican mint and Vodka-tonic gels) Everything about this dish came together perfectly and I loved the little explosions of vodka-tonic from the gels. It is also possible to order this dish a la carte.

- *L'Agneau de l'Aveyron Cuisiné comme un souvenir du Sénégal.* Lamb from Aveyron cooked like a memory of

Senegal. The lamb was exquisitely tender and the sauce had a subtle peanut flavour.

- The cheese and dessert carts are impressive in both quality and quantity. (You'll be wishing for a second stomach!)

One touch I particularly appreciated were the little menu cards supplied with each course. At the end of the meal, the server presents them to you, tied with ribbon to form a little souvenir book. It's the perfect reminder of an epic meal. Restaurant Bon Bon - Avenue de Tervueren 453 (Read my extended review of Restaurant Bon Bon)

Alexandre

Restaurant Alexandre had one Michelin star when I visited but sadly didn't get the nod for 2015. It's a pity, because this female-led restaurant is a gastronomic *tour-de-force*. With Anca Petrescu and Isabelle Arpin at the helm, no detail is overlooked, either in the elegant dining-room or on the plate.

I was charmed by the creative and light-hearted plating (one of our dishes arrived on a tiny sofa) and the flavours lived up to appearances.

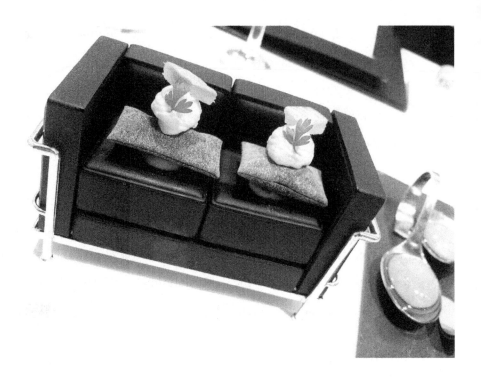

Alexandre offers a great value business lunch on weekdays, or splash out for the evening *Grand Menu,* for an unforgettable meal. Alexandre - Rue du Midi 164

Terborght ‎

While **Restaurant Terborght** isn't strictly in Brussels, it's close enough that it's worth a mention here. This unassuming brick house, in Huizingen, doesn't disclose the foodie delights inside. The interior decor is also subtle earth-tones and not overly styled.

The drama is saved for the food, which arrives on your plate as tiny works of art. The seasonal menus highlight the freshest local produce and the attention to detail is superb.

Terborght currently holds one Michelin-star, and isn't as pricey as its two-star compatriots. However, if you prefer something a little more laid back, the owners also have a brasserie, called Oud Dorp Bistro, featuring Belgian classics. I haven't tried it yet. But if they maintain the calibre of Terborght, it's well worth a visit. Restaurant Terborght - Oud Dorp 16-18, B - 1654 Huizingen

Tram Experience

Normally, the thought of eating in a moving vehicle conjures up images of congealed airline meals or hand-held drive-through snacks. Leave it to Brussels then to come up with a Michelin-starred meal served while touring the city by tram. For the ultimate in unique fine-dining experiences, don't miss the **Tram Experience**.

The Tram Experience was conceived as a temporary event to highlight Brussels' year of gastronomy. It was so popular, they made it a permanent fixture on the summer dining scene.

This is no ordinary trip on public transportation. The tram, dating back to the 1960s, has been completely refitted with sleek white tables and chairs and a customised kitchen, designed by Electrolux. The tables are specially created with cut-outs for glasses, plates and cutlery, to keep things from sliding around. The funky blue and purple lighting and glasses of champagne set the tone for a fun night.

Each evening 34 passengers dine on three courses, while the tram circles Brussels. The journey begins at Place Poelaert and continues up Avenue Louise. From there, the tram continues on to Flagey, Merode, Montgomery, the Tram Museum, Herrmann-Debroux, Boondaal Station, and back to Poelaert, via Buyl. The tram makes no stops but, luckily, there are rest-rooms on-board.

Just as the tram is unique and exclusive, so are the chefs who prepare the menus. Tram Experience diners have feasted on menus designed by Brussels' top chefs, including Michelin-star holders and up-and-coming super-stars. The night I dined on board, the menu was conceived by Pascal Devalkeneer, of Le Chalet de la Forêt. Chefs and menus change regularly on the Tram Experience so there is always something new to try. The Tram Experience (Read my extended review of The Tram Experience)

Belgian Classics

There is no shortage of restaurants and brasseries, in Brussels, featuring traditional Belgian dishes. In fact, faced with so many options, it can be difficult to choose.

In the 'Essential Belgian Foods' section above, I've listed where to go to try specific foods. Some of those restaurants are described here in more detail.

However, if you aren't after a specific dish and are just looking for a restaurant with good Belgian cuisine, both traditional and modern interpretations, any of the restaurants in this section will be an excellent choice.

Jaloa

There are a few great options for dining in the Sainte Catherine neighbourhood. However, when people ask me where to go for great seafood in Brussels, **Jaloa**, and the more casual **Jaloa Brasserie**, are first on the list.

Jaloa itself is elegant fine-dining and a wonderful experience if you are looking to splurge. (Don't miss the fresh oyster bar.) The restaurant only seats 25 people and features tasting menus of four, six, or nine courses.

The Jaloa Brasserie is more cosy and affordable but with the same high level of quality. The menu is à la carte, with the exception of a monthly tasting menu.

Both the restaurant and brasserie feature seasonal, local ingredients and have hidden terraces you can enjoy, during the warmer months.

Jaloa - Sint-Katelijneplein 5

Bozar Brasserie

Brussels' BOZAR Museum is well worth visiting, for its excellent art exhibitions, concerts, and events, like TEDx Brussels. But it's also worth visiting for its gastronomic restaurant, the **BOZAR Brasserie**, headed by Chef David Martin.

The menu changes each month and includes Belgian favourites with a fresh, modern twist. Ingredients are organic and sourced locally when possible, with dashes of international flavours like Basque pork and Anjou pigeon. The prices aren't for the budget conscious, ranging from 20-40 Euros for a main dish. However, the set lunch menus from Tuesday to Friday make a more wallet-friendly option.

Even if you don't spring for a whole meal here, stop in for a coffee and dessert. The speciality of the chef is a dark chocolate 'bomb', filled with creamy, rich praline and accompanied with homemade passion fruit sorbet. The sweet/tart combination is heavenly.

The BOZAR Brasserie doesn't take reservations so go early and be prepared to wait. It's worth it. BOZAR Brasserie – Rue Baron Horta 3

Café Novo

In the city centre, not far from Grand Place, is **Café Novo**; a great place to try classic Belgian dishes, particularly *carbonnade*. This colourfully quirky Belgian café always has an eclectic crowd. The menu is varied and caters well to vegetarians (the falafels are great!) as well as carnivores.

Café Novo is open every day (a rarity in Brussels) and is perfect for a late Sunday brunch. They have a small but sunny back garden that books up quickly. Thursday evenings Novo hosts 'cocktail concerts' so you can enjoy a bit of live music as you dine. <u>Café Novo</u> - Place de la Vieille Halle aux Blés 37

L'Idiot du Village

Nestled on the corner of Rue Blaes and Rue Notre-Seigneur, in the shabby-chic Marolles, is a cosy little secret of in-the-know foodies. It's called **L'Idiot du Village**, but even the village idiot will tell you, it's worth finding this little restaurant.

While the décor is funky (with just a touch of odd) the food is straight-up delicious. The duck and game dishes are heavenly and

L'idiot has a way with scallops. If you are adventurous, order the special of the day, as it's bound to be seasonal and wonderful.

If you want a real taste of 'quirky' Brussels, L'Idiot du Village is not to be missed. L'Idiot isn't open on weekends and it books up quickly so reservations are essential. L'Idiot du Village - Ons-Heerstraat 19 (Read my extended review of L'Idiot du Village)

Belga Queen

For an elegant yet trendy meal in Brussels, featuring great Belgian ingredients, a visit to **Belga Queen** is a must. This restaurant's setting, inside a former bank, is stunning. The period features of the bank remain, but are contrasted by modern elements, like the super-chic bathrooms and the after-hours dance club. There's even a cigar bar inside the old vault.

But the main attraction at Belga Queen is the food. Start your meal with a tower of seafood delights from the oyster and shellfish bar. Just be careful to save room for what's next, as the portions are ample. Main courses range from more seafood (lobster anyone?), to the best Belgian beef, poultry, and game, depending on the season.

My husband, a pork fanatic, declared the pork knuckle one of the best he's ever eaten. Meanwhile, I adore the melting duck breast with red berries. Heaven.

If you have someone to impress, or simply want to be impressed yourself, Belga Queen is a winning choice. The only caveat is due to the large, open-dining concept; it can get quite noisy, meaning it's not the best choice for intimate conversations. Belga Queen Wolvengracht 32

Les Petits Oignons

Les Petits Oignons, a brasserie near Grand Sablon, is an upscale spot to try classic Belgian dishes. The menu is extensive and features traditional favourites like vol-au-vent and steak frites. The set menus feature international cuisine, with additions like risotto and octopus salad.

I particularly recommend the perfectly crispy grey shrimp croquettes and rich and delicious goose foie gras. If you make it through the ample portions, save room to choose from the extensive dessert menu. Les Petits Oignons - Rue de la Régence 25

Peï & Meï

At **Peï & Meï**, a gastronomic bistro, you'll find traditional Belgian favourites as well as international flavours, all presented with precision and the utmost freshness.

The 5-course 'menu surprise' is a bargain at €55, considering the quality and attention to detail. The flavour combinations are truly unique and I found myself 'mmmming' over things I don't normally enjoy (like pickles). The service was exceptionally friendly and helpful, despite the restaurant filling up quickly. Be sure to reserve your table at this one, as the small dining room books up quickly! Restaurant Peï & Meï - 15, Rue de Rollebeek

Slow Food

Brussels is fortunate to have an active branch of the Slow Food movement. Every year, the organization rates restaurants around the city that agree to offer local, clean, and sustainable food. They range from Michelin starred fine-dining, like Restaurant Bon Bon (mentioned above), to budget international fare, like MoMo (mentioned below). There is something for everyone on the Slow Food list, but the following are a few of my stand-out favourites.

Les Filles

Les Filles is a bustling restaurant near Place Sainte Catherine that offers a traditional family-style dining experience. Not only do you eat from communal dishes, whatever happens to be the meal of the day, you sit with strangers (who may even become friends). The organic food is a bit like Grandma's comforting meals – but Grandma never served such good wines! Les Filles - 46 Vieux Marché aux Grains

Brigittines

The cosy **Les Brigittines** wins points for its old-school Art Nouveau architecture, as well as great traditional Belgian food. The chef also highlights local beers from Cantillon and the Brasserie de la Senne

both alongside and even in some of his dishes. Les Brigittines - 5 Place de la Chapelle

La Buvette

I've had so many great dining experiences in Belgium, it's hard to choose a favourite. I can say, without reservation, **La Buvette** is in my top five. This slow food restaurant is warm and classy without feeling overly stuffy or formal.

The concept is simple – one menu, five courses, drinks optional. The ingredients are local, organic, and seasonal. The food is, without a word of exaggeration, divine. The presentations are artistic and beautiful and the flavour profiles are complex without being confusing. Each and every ingredient shines through.

The best part - the menu is €49. Are you making reservations yet? A rarity in Brussels, La Buvette also caters to special diets, provided you let them know in advance. Restaurant La Buvette - Chaussee d'Alsemberg 108 (Read my extended review of La Buvette)

Le Mess

In addition to being a fun, quirky place to dine, inside a former prison, **Le Mess** focuses on slow food versions of traditional Belgian dishes. There is a strong emphasis on sustainable seafood and the organic lamb comes from the Gaume region of Wallonia. Le Mess even offers a 'Veggie Thursday' featuring a vegetarian lunch. <u>Le Mess</u> - Boulevard Louis Schmidt 1

Le Café des Spores

If you love all things fungus, **Café des Spores** is your restaurant. Owned by the folks who own La Buvette (above), everything on the menu features mushrooms – and that includes a cheese course and dessert. The creations, cooked up in the open kitchen, are all delightful. Request a seat on the upper level and you can watch your dinner being cooked below. The only reason not to visit this innovative restaurant is if you are allergic to mushrooms, in which case, I'm very sorry for you. <u>Café des Spores</u> - Chaussee D'Alsemberg 103

Wine Bar Sablon

On the bustling Rue Haute, in the heart of the quirky Marolles district, is **Le Wine Bar**. Located in a typical 17th century house, as the name suggests, the main feature is wine, but that is certainly not the only thing on offer.

The menu is short and heavy on meat dishes, but each one is prepared with care and attention. The beef cheeks braised in red wine melt in your mouth and the owner hand-makes the selection of charcuteries.

The service is excellent and knowledgeable and there are plenty of wines available by the glass and, of course, by the bottle. This is one of my 'not to be missed' destinations for both food and wine in Brussels. Le Wine Bar - Rue Haute 198

International Cuisine

The international food scene, in Brussels, has expanded exponentially, in the past ten years or so. This is great news for visitors and local expats looking for exotic flavours or a taste of home.

When I first arrived in Belgium, the most exotic thing available was extremely westernized 'Chinese' food, in gloppy, bland sauces. As a general rule, Belgians (and in fact most Northern Europeans) aren't fans of spicy foods, so even dishes labelled 'hot' were often bland

and tasteless. And while plenty of these sorts of places still exist, just about every world cuisine is represented in Brussels now, by an authentic restaurant, if you know where to look.

The other great thing about many of these new, international restaurants, is that they offer affordable dining options and a number of them also fall into the 'Cheap Eats' category below.

La Mamma

For me, **La Mamma** is, hands down, the best Italian restaurant in Brussels. In addition to a terrific Italian wine and grappa list, La Mamma features fresh Italian pasta and meat dishes. Many of their ingredients are imported from Italy and there are always seasonal menu selections. The portions are hearty and I never quite make it to the scrumptious looking desserts.

The atmosphere is so cosy, you almost forget you're on the bustling Place St. Josse. With Italian being spoken in the kitchen and a heaping plate of Italy on the table before you, you are transported to *la dolce vita*. La Mamma - Place Saint-Josse 9

La Piola

La Piola is a close runner-up for my favourite Italian restaurant in Brussels. I love the extremely warm and professional service. The portions are huge. It's affordable and it has a young and friendly atmosphere.

The restaurant is located in the hip and trendy Chatelain neighbourhood. While restaurants seem to come and go in the area like passing trains, La Piola has stood the test of time.

On a hot summer evening, there is no better pleasure than enjoying Aperol spritzes on the cosy walled terrace. But the number one reason I love La Piola: Hot. Melted. Cheese. Seriously, if you go, order the Scamorza starter. This smoked buffalo mozzarella is melted into a pan of zesty tomato sauce and the result is a mess of molten, smoky, cheese goodness. You're welcome. <u>La Piola</u> - Rue du Page 2

Sale Pepe Rosemarino

Like many of the hidden gems in Brussels, you could easily pass by the tiny **Sale Pepe Rosemarino** Italian restaurant, near Ave. Louise. Inside the shabby-chic interior, delightful smells emanate from the kitchen. The tiny dining-room fills quickly, with regulars. These are two very good indications, great food will follow.

And follow it does. The handmade pasta is velvety and delicious. This is authentic Italian, prepared with care and attention to detail - just the way Mama would make it. **Sale Pepe Rosemarino** - Rue Berckmans 98

Tasty Corner

There's a lot of great international food in the St. Josse neighbourhood, but as Brussels' smallest (and poorest) commune, few tourists venture here. It's a pity for foodies to miss out on such great quality and variety. One of my favourites is the tiny, but wonderful, **Tasty Corner**, a block from Place St. Josse. This little Lebanese restaurant is always packed with workers from the surrounding office buildings, for weekday lunches.

Absolutely everything here is made from scratch, each morning, by the three generations of women who work here. They are friendly and passionate about the great food they serve, and are happy to help with explanations.

The menu includes a variety of wraps and sandwiches (the falafels are the best I've had anywhere) and 'sampler plates' heaped with various salads and grilled meats. For the adventurous, or indecisive, order the plate of the day (even if you have no idea what it is) as I often do. You'll discover wonderful new flavours your taste buds will thank you for.

Tasty Corner is open for lunch all week long, for dining in or take-away. (Do not confuse it with the take-away counter by the same name at the Arts-loi metro station. It is NOT the same.) Tasty Corner - 86 Chaussée de Louvain

Chez Oki

Chez Oki has been open since 2004; old age for a fine-dining restaurant in Brussels, especially one in the Ixelles neighbourhood.

Chez Oki is French and Japanese fusion, a combination that could go horribly wrong. However, here it is done so right; it seems like a match made in heaven. Chef Haruki Oki was born in Japan and trained in Michelin-starred restaurants in Paris. He marries both of these culinary traditions seamlessly in his dishes.

When I visited, I was taken on a surprise 4-course culinary journey from Tokyo to Paris and back, while remaining seated in the perfectly Zen dining room in Brussels. A blur of foie gras, sushi, tartar, dumplings, and lamb, were presented with care and precision. Every dish tasted familiar, yet was completely innovative, at the same time.

This wonderful restaurant doesn't fall into the 'Cheap Eats' category, but, if you enjoy creative fusion food, it is well worth the splurge for a truly unique and enjoyable meal. <u>Chez Oki</u> - 62, Rue Lesbroussart

Nid Savoureux

I had all but given up on eating at 'Chinese' restaurants in Belgium after a series of disappointments. Even those charging high prices and touting 'authentic' menus, had been woefully bland and generic.

That changed when a friend, who had lived in China, introduced me to the tiny, unassuming **Nid Savoureux**. The husband and wife team hail from Northern China, and the dishes they serve are not those you see on typical European 'Chinese' restaurants - thank goodness!

This is one restaurant where, when they list a dish as spicy, you can see plenty of chili peppers on your plate!

While I've never had a bad dish at Nid Savoureux, I highly recommend the sautéed noodles with beef, chicken in spicy sauce, and the homemade dumplings. The portions are very generous and the friendly owners are happy to box up any left-overs to take away.

The prices are unbeatable, making it a favourite of local students at lunch, but evening services tend to be quiet, which means you'll have the tiny staff's full attention. Le Nid Savoureux - Rue de la Cambre 325 (Read my extended review of Le Nid Savoureux)

MoMo

MoMo is one of a new breed of 'niche' restaurants popping up around Brussels. They have an extremely limited menu, but what they do, they do very well, using only the freshest ingredients and adhering to slow food principles.

The star of the show is the MoMo, a Tibetan steamed dumpling, filled with meat or vegetables. These handmade dumplings can be ordered on their own, or as part of a combo, including soup and steamed vegetables.

A meal here is virtually guilt-free as it is sustainable, healthy, and easy on your wallet too. Oh, and it is exceptionally delicious! MoMo - 27 Rue Defacqz

Knees to Chin

I LOVE spring rolls. But, I'll admit, I was sceptical about a whole restaurant dedicated to rice paper rolls. But I'm now a **Knees to Chin** convert and, if you enjoy fresh Asian flavours, you will be too.

The concept is simple – there are eight fresh and healthy spring rolls to choose from. You can order them a la carte, or as part of a menu, with rice or salad. There are also sides of noodle salad and dim sum that are great for sharing.

Everything is made from scratch on-site, including a variety of homemade sauces. While there are typically chicken, beef, and seafood options, my favourite is actually a vegetarian roll, featuring sweet potato, pineapple, fresh mint, and avocado sauce.

Not only are the spring rolls healthy and very affordable, they are virtually gluten and lactose free (great for special diets!). Knees to Chin is definitely one to try. <u>Knees to Chin</u> - Rue de Livourne 125

Pho Pho

Pho Pho calls itself Vietnamese fast food, but this is so much fresher and tastier than fast food as we know it. You order at the counter, and choose from a variety of soups and starters, then take a seat in the brightly coloured and comfortable seating area. Then you sit back and wait for the steaming bowls of hot soup to arrive.

Pho Pho's soups are HUGE, fresh and delicious. Like in Vietnam, the fresh elements like coriander, lime, chili peppers, and bean sprouts are served on the side, both so they stay crispy and fresh, but also so you can customize your Pho to perfection. Pho Pho Vietnamese Fast Food - Rue de la Paix 27 and Boulevard du Jardin Botanique 6

Samourai Ramen

Like Pho Pho, the star of the short **Samourai Ramen** menu is soup. And this soup is certainly one of the best I've had outside Asia.

The original Samouraï Ramen is located just behind the De Brouckere metro, on Rue Fossé-aux-loups, right beside the original Samouraï Japanese restaurant (another fine choice but much more expensive). The dining room is cosy, simple and bright, owing to the large wrap-around windows. Or, head for the brand new location in Ixelles, which is much larger with a bright, modern vibe.

The menu is extremely short – perfectly so. There is nothing but ramen, edamamé (steamed soya beans) and gyoza (Japanese dumplings), with a short selection of drinks and two Japanese desserts.

For the ramen, you can choose from a selection of three broths: miso, shôyu (a soya sauce based broth), and tonkotsu (made from pork bones). In addition to the noodles and veggies that come in your broth, you can choose to add additional toppings, like breaded chicken or shrimp, sliced pork, or a hard-boiled egg.

The huge, steaming bowls arrive quickly, and the broth is rich and deeply flavourful. The service is friendly but seating is very limited. Samouraï Ramen - Rue Fossé-aux-loups 28 and Rue Capitaine Crespel 1 (Read my extended review of Samouri Ramen)

King Kong

King Kong is another unique 'niche' restaurant, this time featuring Peruvian-style sandwiches. Like Pho Pho, it offers counter service, with take-away, but there is a lovely seating area, at the back, where you can enjoy your sandwich hot from the grill.

The choices feature rotisserie chicken, available in sandwich form or on the bone, roasted pork, salads, roasted potatoes, and even ceviche. I thoroughly enjoyed my Chicharron sandwich, which was a full meal, even before I added the perfect roasted potatoes.

King Kong is one of the budget, hipster hangouts in Brussels, so you may have to wade your way through ironic suspenders and fedoras, but it's worth it for a quick, healthy, affordable meal on the go. King Kong - 227 Chaussée de Charleroi

MexiGo

An authentic Mexican restaurant is one giant hole in the international cuisine tapestry, in Brussels. Currently, it is only filled by dreary chain buffet 'Tex-Mex' not even worth mentioning (other than to say avoid it or risk food-poisoning).

The only place in town to get an authentic taste of Mexico is the tiny **MexiGo** shop, in Ixelles. While not a sit down restaurant, MexiGo does offer fresh-made burritos, fried tacos and empanadas, as well as MexiGo's delicious guacamole, tomatillo, and jalapeno cheddar dips. If you miss Mexican, MexiGo should be your destination. MexiGo - 47 Francois Dons (See the 'International Ingredients' section below for more on the MexiGo shop)

Curry

As a foodie expert for Belgium, one of my most frequently asked questions is 'where can I get a good Indian curry in Brussels?' While London used to be my ironic reply, Brussels finally has good Indian restaurant options for curry-lovers. Hallelujah! If there is one cuisine I love above all others, it is Indian.

One great option for truly home-cooked Indian cuisine is through **Bookalokal** (See What to Do below). A number of Indian expats cater to the international community, longing for decent curry, by cooking them at home. If you are open to meeting new people, this is a great option.

In terms of restaurants, rather than list all of the Indian options, in Brussels you shouldn't bother with, I'll give you the **one** you absolutely should try - **Indus Pride South Indian Restaurant** (part of the Sibys Restaurants group).

I first learned about Indus Pride from an Indian foodie friend. If she said it was good, I knew I had to try it. A month before leaving Belgium to travel full-time, I was able to dine there. The saddest part was learning Indus Pride has actually been around since 2007! I could have saved myself countless disappointing curries, if only I had known about Indus Pride sooner.

I believe Indus Pride's location is keeping it a local secret. Tucked at the bottom of an apartment block, in Woluwe St. Lambert, it's not the most obvious spot for an Indian restaurant. The interior doesn't look like your typical Indian restaurant either. The décor is refreshingly modern and elegant. While there are a few nods to Indian culture in the accents, you're not hit over the head with it.

What **is** truly Indian and authentic is the food. The menu is extensive, with plenty of options for carnivores and vegetarians alike. While you'll find the half dozen curries recognised at every Indian restaurant, there are many lesser-known dishes as well. Indus Pride specialises in Southern Indian cuisine (my personal favourite), including my favourite crispy treat, the dosa.

If you are looking for an excellent Indian restaurant in Brussels, this is it. It's easily accessible by car and about a 10-15 minute walk from Rodebeek metro station. The Sibys group operates a number of restaurants in Brussels and Zaventem. If they all are as good as Indus Pride, it's worth seeking them out! Indus Pride (Sibys) - 59 Avenue Marcel Thiry (Read more on the Best Indian Curry Restaurants in Brussels)

The Burger Wars

Hamburgers may not seem like an exotic international food, but when I first arrived in Brussels a decent burger was almost nonexistent. Oh sure, you could find a fast-food joint on every corner, but a burger made from fresh ingredients and cooked to perfection was as elusive as the Holy Grail.

This is all hard to believe as you walk around Brussels now. It seems like there's a trendy burger bar every few metres. Burger-mania has overtaken the city and the question of who makes the best one is as hotly contested as the *frite* issue.

In my opinion no one does burgers better than **Cool Bun**.

Cool Bun uses only organic ingredients and makes all of their sauces from scratch. The variety of toppings is endless: Gorgonzola, caramelized onions, guacamole, jalapenos, even foie gras. If you have a gigantic appetite, order the Big Ben - a double burger with lettuce, oven dried tomatoes, cheddar, onions rings, avocado, jalapenos, and bacon.

If you're not in the mood for a burger, try the Texan BBQ menu. Chicken, ribs, and beef are all smoked in house using home-made sauces. It's carnivore heaven.

But for me, the best thing about Cool Bun is the onion rings (another rarity in Belgium). These huge rings of golden goodness are super crispy on the outside and juicy on the inside. While everyone else is busy arguing over the best burger in town, I'll have the onion rings all to myself. Cool Bun - Rue Berckmans 34 & Rue Stevin 168

(Read my extended review of Cool Bun and the Texas BBQ menu)

My runner up to Cool Bun is the **Urban Cook food truck**. I love their Rock burger, with Roquefort and bacon. Andrew is a big fan of the Classique, with cheese, and we both enjoy the Tartuffo, truffle burger. The thick cut fries make a nice addition and all of the sauces are homemade. Urban Cook also has some of the best burger buns we've had in Belgium. Because the truck's location is always changing, <u>check their website for details</u>.

If you can't make it to Cool Bun or chase down Urban Cook, there are a few other decent burger restaurants to try.

[There are a few big names who are notably absent from this list. Despite having big followings, I find the burgers sub-standard and/or the service lacking. The restaurants in the list below offer top quality ingredients and great service.]

- Manhattan's Burgers - Order your New York-style burgers at the counter and enjoy - Avenue Louise 164
- Les Super Filles du Tram - A large selection in a relaxed atmosphere - Rue Lesbroussart 22
- Houtsiplou - Fun and funky with a burger for everyone (even vegetarians) - 9 Place Rouppe
- Le Tram de Boisfort - It's outside of the centre, but worth it for a great burger in a unique setting inside an old tram - Place Payfa, 1170 Watermael-Boitsfort

Cheap Eats

When I first arrived in Brussels, dining out was hard on the wallet. The only good, budget-friendly options were the less-than-healthy frites, and fast-food chains (a no-go for a slow-foodie, like me.) Luckily, the demand for fresh **and** affordable food in the capital has created a new movement we can see in both the rise of food-trucks, and in healthy fast-food options.

As I explained above, many of the new niche-style, international restaurants are also great budget options. If you jumped immediately to this section, be sure to check out the following international options above:

- Tasty Corner (Lebanese)
- Le Nid Savoureux (Chinese)
- MoMo (Tibetan)
- Knees to Chin (Spring rolls)
- Pho Pho (Vietnamese)
- Samourai Ramen (Japanese)
- King Kong (Peruvian)
- MexiGo (Mexican)

Bookalokal (listed under What to Do) is another way to enjoy a full, home-cooked meal that is easy on the budget.

Below I list a few more options for delicious food that won't cost a bundle.

Noordzee / Mer du Nord

If you are looking for a uniquely Brussels foodie experience, you absolutely can't miss **Noordzee / Mer du Nord**; Even the name is in two of the official Belgian languages.

This seafood counter has no seats, but that doesn't stop locals from flocking to this 'seafood bar' at lunchtime. Noordzee isn't even really a restaurant but a fish-seller that happens to sell some of the best seafood snacks in the city.

I've listed them above, as where to find the best grey shrimp croquettes and their fried calamari is crispy perfection. The fish soup is incredible on a cold day. The mussels, shrimps, calamari and oysters are all as fresh as it gets and, washed down with a chilled glass of white wine or champagne, make the perfect decadent lunch. The menu depends on the season and the catch of the day.

In the summer, you can enjoy your lunch in the square, while you people-watch or do as the locals do and enjoy a snack while you wait, as your seafood order is prepared for you to take home. Mer du Nord / Noordzee - Rue Ste Catherine 45

Mamma Roma

Pizza is often a traveller's go-to for a cheap, filling, and reasonably healthy meal. There are loads of pizza options in Brussels but for original, fresh, and affordable selections, local chain, **Mamma**

Roma is the best. Mamma Roma offers a selection of pre-made pizza options, with and without meat (my favourite is the potato truffle pizza). You simply point at the pizzas you'd like, and the server will cut you off a hunk and grill it in the pizza oven. You can mix and match your pizzas as much as you want and then you pay by weight (the pizza's, not yours.) Mamma Roma offers a great lunch deal; 2 slices of pizza and a drink for €8.90. Mamma Roma has locations around the city, including one in the centre at 17 rue du Pont de la Carpe.

Arcadi café

L'Arcadie is one of the only exceptions to the "don't eat near Grand Place" rule. Located at the end of the Galleries Saint Hubert covered shopping arcade, this café is always packed, with both tourists and Brussels locals. The pasta and meals are good but what locals really come is for is the quiche. It is made fresh daily and the varieties are endless. There are always plenty of options for vegetarians as well. It's one of the few cheap and healthy(ish) restaurants only steps from Grand Place. Try to save room for the homemade cakes and tarts (or come back for a slice and coffee after you walk around central Brussels.) **L'Arcadie** - Rue d'Arenberg 1B

Bia Mara

With a huge community of British expats in Brussels, it's hard to believe there was no decent place to get fish 'n chips, in the capital. But, until the opening of **Bia Mara**, this was a sad fact.

Seafood lovers in Brussels can now rejoice. Not only is the fish fresh (the owner regularly rejects seafood orders that aren't up to his high standard) and the menu creative (Spicy tempura salmon anyone?) but everything is sustainable.

You would expect such an establishment to be pricey, but Bia Mara is made for the budget conscious. For roughly 10 euro you get 2 large pieces of fresh fish (your choice of fish and style) with a mound of thick cut fries. You also choose one of 6 delicious sauces and a flavoured salt for your chips. Everything is made in house from organic and local ingredients.

Vegetarians and carnivores aren't forgotten at Bia Mara either, with chicken and vegetarian options available.

It is located just steps from Grand Place so you have no excuse not to visit. <u>Bia Mara</u> - Rue du Marche Aux Poulets 41 (Read my <u>extended review of Bia Mara</u>)

Special Diets

In a country where bacon is considered a vegetable and a meal without bread is unthinkable, Belgium can be a culinary mine-field for people with special dietary needs. Luckily, in Brussels, things are beginning to change. Slowly, awareness of people with special dietary needs is growing and there are more and more options for vegetarians, vegans, and gluten intolerants. (Read my extended listing of <u>where to eat and shop in Brussels with special diets</u>)

Vegetarian Restaurants

There are only a handful of truly vegetarian restaurants in Brussels. While vegetarian and vegan dishes aren't necessarily gluten-free, there is often a better awareness of food intolerances in these restaurants. Special requests for gluten-free meals tend to be better received in vegetarian restaurants in Brussels, than elsewhere. I would recommend the following:

- Dolma
- La Tsampa
- Shanti
- TAN (See Bloggers Top Picks below)

You can also refer to the Happy Cow listing for more vegetarian friendly restaurants in Brussels.

Gluten Free Brussels

Restaurant dining can be challenging for celiacs and the gluten intolerant, particularly in traditional Belgian restaurants. Bread and pasta are prevalent and sauces are often thickened with wheat flour. While choices of meat, salads, and (thank goodness) Belgian frites are normally gluten-free, wheat can be hiding in unexpected places so it's always a good idea to chat with your server.

Asian Restaurants – Keep in mind that many Thai, Japanese, Indian, and other Asian foods are naturally rice based and gluten-free. Just be sure to ask about any extra additives.

Il Veliero Italian Restaurant – Italian certainly isn't the first cuisine that comes to mind when you're looking for gluten-free options. However, this restaurant, just off of Place Jourdan, has a full gluten-free menu including pizza and pasta. They also offer lactose free pizza. I dined there, with a friend, and she was very happy with her gluten-free pizza. My regular old wheat-based pizza was great too. Rue Général Leman 15

Toscana 21 and Ricotta & Parmesan are also Italian restaurants, with the same owner. Both offer gluten-free pasta on request.

For quick and easy lunch options, the Exki chain offers a variety of salads and dishes including quinoa and other gluten-free grains.

Soul

As a confirmed omnivore, it may seem odd, one of my favourite restaurants in Brussels is listed in the vegetarian and special diets section. However, **Soul** has been at the top of my list for years now, and it's a great place to visit if you have one or more special dietary requirements in your party.

While neither strictly vegetarian nor gluten-free, Soul is macrobiotic, meaning everything is organic, locally sourced, where possible, and the chef is aware of the effects ingredients have on your body and mood.

Soul caters to a variety of special diets, including gluten and lactose intolerance, food allergies, and vegan and vegetarian diets. Just speak to your server before ordering.

But even if you enjoy eating everything, as I do, Soul has a great shabby-chic atmosphere, the servers are friendly and well-versed in the menu items, and the food is delicious and sustaining. Reservations are strongly recommended. <u>Soul</u> - Rue de la Samaritaine 20

Breakfast and Brunch

Typically, Belgians aren't big breakfast eaters. Much like France, you'll be hard pressed to find more than a croissant or pain-au-chocolate to accompany your morning coffee. If you're looking for a big English or American-style breakfast, these are few and far between.

That said, in recent years, Bruxellois have embraced the concept of Brunch and more and more restaurants are offering large mid-day meals, particularly on Sunday.

L'Orangerie du Parc d'Egmont

The most well-known, extensive, and expensive brunch in Brussels is also one of the most hidden away, deep in the heart of the Parc d'Egmont.

This little green jewel of a park is tucked between the Boulevard de Waterloo and the petit Sablon, behind The Hotel (see Hotels section below). Unless you specifically set out to find it, you would never even know it is there. Once inside, it's hard to believe you are right beside the ring road.

In the heart of the park sits the **Orangerie** restaurant, in a neoclassical building. It has a huge terrace, where you can sit and enjoy the sights and sounds of the park. While the Orangerie is a lovely spot to stop for lunch or a coffee-break on any sunny day, on Saturdays and Sundays, it is a brunch extravaganza.

The offerings include pastries and breads, cheeses, cured meats, smoked salmon and mackerel, a wide variety of salads and grilled vegetables, hot pasta, and an omelet and crepe bar. Juices are also included but hot drinks are not.

The Orangerie's brunch isn't cheap. At €29 per person, it's a splurge (so eat light the night before). However, brunch at the Orangerie is a great way to spend a decadent, sunny, Sunday afternoon in the heart of the city, and yet still feel like you are away from it all. L'Orangerie du Parc D'Egmont - Parc d'Egmont

Gaudron

Away from the busy city centre on pretty Place Brugmann, in Brussels Ixelles neighbourhood is local foodie favourite, **Gaudron**. Gaudron is many things: a catering company, a restaurant, a party venue, a deli, and a relaxing terrace to grab a drink after work.

Gaudron was one of the first of Brussels' restaurants to catch on to the Sunday brunch concept and it remains popular. Gaudron's brunch (available on week-ends and holidays) includes a baguette, pastry, butter and jam, ham and cheese, fresh fruit juice, a hot drink and one egg cooked however you like, for 20 Euro. You can also order à la carte choosing from fresh pastries, egg dishes, or lunchtime favourites, like salads, toasted sandwiches and hamburgers. There are fresh squeezed juices and homemade smoothies and milkshakes.

It's a loud, bustling sort of place that's filled with groups of all ages and is family-friendly. With a huge selection of salads in the deli, it's vegetarian and vegan friendly too.

If you want an authentic Brussels neighbourhood feel, it's worth escaping the centre for a trip to Gaudron. Gaudron - Place Georges Brugmann 3, 1050 Ixelles

Café de la Press

With its retro-chic interior and free wifi, **Café de la Press** is a favourite with the hipster crowd in Brussels. You'll find an equal mix of lunching expats, location independent travellers, trendy young Belgians, and a whole lot of MacBooks.

On a sunny weekend, the sidewalk terrace is heaving, and on a chilly winter Sunday, you may have to fight for a table. It's worth braving the crowd for the bagel sandwiches, a rare treat in Brussels. You'll find them topped with traditional brunch favourites like bacon and eggs, or you can opt for something a bit different, like chicken and avocado.

It wouldn't be a proper Belgian café, if they couldn't get the coffee right – and they do. Whether you prefer a perfect, tiny, rich espresso, or a dessert-in-a-glass caramel macchiato, you can find it here.

Brunch is served every Sunday and reservations are required. Café de la Press - 493 Avenue Louise

Peck 47

If you can't wait for the weekend to enjoy an egg-filled breakfast, relative newcomer, **Peck 47**, might be just the ticket.

Peck 47 is a cosy little sandwich shop, just steps from the Grand Place. While the sandwiches are tasty, there are also some nice budget brunch options. If you love poached eggs, then this is your joint!

I love Peck 47 for their drinks. While they offer inventive cocktails, it's actually the non-alcoholic beverages I crave: big, thick smoothies, organic juices, great coffee, and lovely herbal teas. They even have a tea called Alison's Secret Garden – how could it not be a winner? <u>Peck 47</u> - Rue Marche Aux Poulets 47

Drinks

If you are looking to enjoy Belgian beer, be sure to check out the 'Big 4' section of the 'Belgian Foods' chapter. For all other drink options, you've come to the right place.

Just because Belgians love their beer, doesn't mean there are no great bars catering to other drinks. Cocktails are popular in Brussels, and new bars dedicated to specific alcohols are popping up all over town.

Belgians are also big wine drinkers, although the concept of wine bars is relatively new, owing to the preference of wine *with* the meal. One of the best places to enjoy both is at the aptly named Wine Bar (listed in the Slow Food section).

Below are a few great places to grab a drink, other than beer, in the capital.

Aksum Coffee House

If you're as serious about coffee as I am, you'll find your perfect cup at **Aksum Coffee House**. Tucked in a quaint corner building, near Grand Place, Aksum Coffee House takes its name from a town in Northern Ethiopia, where coffee was first discovered.

These folks know their beans. They source organic coffee direct from specific farms, in two regions of Ethiopia, to roast to exacting specifications. These are some of the finest coffees in the world, and you'll taste the difference immediately.

The added bonus - service with a big smile and plenty of knowledge on offer, if you need help choosing your perfect cup. <u>Aksum Coffee House</u> - Rue des Eperonniers 60

Etiquette

Wine bars are a recent phenomenon in Brussels, but in the past few years, they have been popping up around town like mushrooms after the rain. Back in those pre-wine bar days, I dreamed someone would open my perfect wine bar and suddenly, they did. It's called **Etiquette** and it is wine-lover heaven.

Etiquette is many things: a shop, where you can purchase wines by the bottle; a restaurant, where you can eat tasty tapas-style treats (the braised pork belly is pure heaven); and of course, it's a wine bar, where you can drink excellent wines by the glass.

Etiquette uses an innovative chip-card system for the wine bar. You pay a small deposit and are given a card, which you load money onto. You then peruse the wines available in their seven wine fridges and select a wine to sample. You insert your chip card into the machine, select your wine, and the size of glass you'd like. The machine dispenses the correct amount into your wine glass and debits the cost from your card. It's a vending machine for grown-ups.

The wines are excellent, as is the food, the staff is super friendly and helpful and the atmosphere is relaxed and cosy. In short, it's my dream wine bar come to life. Etiquette - Emile De Motlaan 19

L'Archiduc

L'Archiduc is Brussels best loved venue for live jazz. This Art Deco cocktail bar is a favourite, for Saturday night's 'After Shopping Jazz' and Sunday's 'Round About 5' live music.

The club has been in existence since 1937, and under its current ownership since 1985. With its classic atmosphere, it's like stepping back in time, as you sink into one of the cozy benches. The well-stocked bar carries everything from whiskeys to champagnes but is best known for its cocktails.

L'Archiduc is open from 5pm 'til late' (generally 5am), every night except Christmas Eve. Press the buzzer by the door to be admitted, order a champagne cocktail, pull up a chair by the grand piano, sit back and enjoy the music. L'Archiduc - Antoine Dansaertstraat 6

The Bar

While there are many cocktail bars in Brussels, I tend not to frequent them. The problem is not the cocktails themselves, (although I have been served my fair share of watery mojitos), but the atmosphere. Rather than stimulating conversation, I normally find myself shouting over loud (usually bad) music. I enjoy trashy dance music as much as the next person, but when I go out for a drink, it's normally to catch up with friends; an impossible task, over a bass beat.

I'll be the first to admit, a hotel bar in my own city would not normally spring to mind, when I'm looking to go out for a drink – until I discovered The Bar, at the luxurious The Hotel. (Yes that really is THE name.)

While The Bar certainly isn't a budget option, if you are looking for a stylish place to unwind and be served a perfect cocktail, The Bar is **The** place to go. Enjoy a perfectly prepared Bellini, martini, or leave it up to the creativity of Fabrizio and his excellently trained staff. The Bar @ The Hotel - Boulevard de Waterloo 38 (See Where to Stay, below, for more on The Hotel)

Ginothèque

Once reserved for British expats *of a certain age*, Gin and Tonics are suddenly all the rage in Brussels, a fad of which I'm a fan. The best G&T I've enjoyed in Brussels, thus far, was served at the aptly named **Ginothèque**, at the Radisson Blu Royal hotel, in the city centre.

The bar is located in the bright and open atrium, close to both the Atrium Restaurant and Sea Grill (See 'The Stars' above), making it perfect for a pre (or post) dinner cocktail.

The Ginothèque has a good variety of high-end gins and half a dozen kinds of tonic. You can mix and match your own or ask the bartender to create something to your taste. I left myself in the mixologist's capable hands and was definitely happy with the result!

It's also possible to order a variety of tapas and snacks with your drinks, or just cozy up on the sofa-style seats with a coffee and enjoy the atmosphere. The Ginothèque @ Radisson Blu Royal - Rue du Fosse-aux-Loups 47 (See Where to Stay, below, for more on the Radisson Blu Royal)

Brussels' Bloggers' Top Restaurant Picks

One of the best things about being a foodie in Brussels is you are definitely not alone. Belgians and expats alike share a passion for all things edible in the city and there's no place better to experience this, than online. There are so many excellent blogs dedicated to the Belgian food scene and these passionate food writers have their finger on the pulse of the latest and greatest places to eat in Brussels. Not only are they knowledgeable, but the Brussels food blogger community is one of the kindest, most open groups of people I've ever met, and I'm honoured to call so many of them friends.

As no one could possibly eat at every restaurant in Brussels (I know; I've tried my best), I've asked some of my favourite Brussels foodies for help and, below, they each share one of their top restaurant picks for Brussels. In addition, I've shared links to their websites and I urge you to visit each and every one. You're bound to find so much information on eating in Brussels, you may never want to leave!

Mamy Louise

From **Monika Lamba** - Regular contributor to CheeseWeb.eu

If you are looking for a restaurant with affordable Michelin quality food, Mamy Louise is the answer. I have visited on multiple occasions, and the food has always been of exceptional quality and the service pleasant. The restaurant serves contemporary French-Belgian cuisine, but the flavours are authentic.

Mamy Louise has several locations around Brussels and neighbouring areas. The restaurant has a neo-retro décor, with the wall pieces giving an almost American atmosphere. The seating is both intimate and comfortable and there is also a small terrace open in the summer.

I have always found the service pleasing and the concierge is always happy to explain the menu. Though the choice of drinks is limited, the house wines are quite decent. The bread, served with the wine, is exceptional and usually comes with a complimentary appetizer. The menu features both classic dishes and Mamy's unique preparations. The starters are a great reflection of Belgian food and produce, the salads fresh and crisp, and the seafood and meat quality is phenomenal. The essence here is simple, straightforward cuisine cooked with the best fresh ingredients.

One of my fondest memories is tucking into a delicious piece of lamb, cooked to perfection, accompanied by a coconut milk sauce infused with the richness of dry fruits. On another occasion, I ordered a flavourful confit duck leg, which was tender on the inside and nicely done on the outside. The restaurant also offers pasta and risottos, bearing the same unmistakable Mamy standard.

All things considered, Mamy Louise is a must-visit, for a special meal. Individual dishes, can vary from 15 to 35 euros, but it is money well spent. You know you will be treated well, the food will be excellent, and the experience sublime. Mamy Louise - Several locations in Brussels.

Le Bugatti

From **Maxine Chowles** - Blogs in English, at Why I Am Not Skinny

Truly delicious Belgian dishes, friendly service, and easily accessible - **Le Bugatti**, in Ixelles, is our 'go-to' restaurant. It's where we take our visiting friends, it's the place we recommend to tourists, and of course it's our favourite venue to celebrate date night! Open since 1988, they really do know what they are doing!

My husband always orders the sausages & stoemp (a vegetable & potato mash), while I always order the Chateaubriand (Irish Angus Beef) steak. The rest of the menu is perfectly Belgian: eels in green sauce, beef stew made with Trappist dark beer, mussels, rabbit Kriek stew, and, of course, the obligatory homemade croquettes. (I recommend ordering the mixed duet as a starter, with one croquette of grey shrimps from the North Sea and one parmesan cheese croquette, both perfectly deep-fried and served with fried parsley).

All this can be enjoyed as you gaze upon the murals… cars, cars, and more cars. Why? Because this used to be a private garage, from 1885.

One thing to note is they don't take credit or debit cards - so be armed with cash! Le Bugatti - 4 Rue Jacques Jordaens

Au Stekerlapatte

From **Andreea Gulacsi** - Blogs in English, at On Food and Wine

Au Stekerlapatte is a restaurant that was on my list to try for a very long time. I was told by various friends, if I wanted to try out true local Brussels cuisine, this is the place to go to. In its glory days, Au Stekerlapatte was the go-to address for the Brussels artsy scene – actors, radio and TV journalists, press.

The restaurant is set on a back street, between Saint Gilles and the Marolles, behind the Palace of Justice. It takes a bit of an effort to find the place! The upside however, is once you do find it, you don't really want to leave.

Although recently refurbished, the owner has kept all the original features, which are typical Belgian Art Nouveau inspired – wrought iron bar, stained glass dome, wooden panel seating. The overall impression is a very cozy traditional Brussels brasserie.

The menu offers an intriguing combination of Belgian food, with Marolles inspired dishes and the occasional 'outsider'. Personally, I don't see the need for Asian influenced dishes in such a traditional place. The attractiveness of Au Stekerlapatte is, by far, its Belgianism ... not its curry.

Back to the food - It doesn't get more local than this! Starters include the terrine maison, or the typical Marolles dish of bloempanch (black pudding). Mains are equally interesting (and dare I say more than

104

enough to make a meal) from steak frites to a roasted knuckle of ham.

Even with the maitre d's detailed introduction to the local cuisine, it takes a brave soul to dive into the Marolles dishes. I opted for the grilled mussels as a starter and *boulettes* (meatballs) for my main. My husband went fishy for his starter (squid) and then ordered the 'Marolles' pigs trotters for his main. To pair with our food, we chose different glasses of wine, as Au Stekerlapatte offers a very decent wine selection by the glass.

Even if you're full, I dare you to resist the most scrumptious mousse of speculoos you've ever had! I've had my fair share of Belgian desserts and I can honestly say a visit to Au Stekerlapatte is justified by this mousse alone - or the café gourmand, which in my opinion was a 100% win-win, as I literally had a mini piece of each of their signature desserts. Dead-o-dessert heaven!

The maitre d' was a quirky character, as well as a great talker, and we learned a lot about the neighbourhood, the food history of the Marolles, and generally about Au Stekerlapatte's history; including the origin of the name, which is Marolles dialect meaning to swim in two directions at the same time. It was a true pleasure and the reason I adore this kind of Brussels restaurant where tradition still lives on.
Au Stekerlapatte - Rue de Praitre 4

La Meilleure Jeunesse

From **Maxine Chowles** - Blogs in English, at <u>Why I Am Not Skinny</u>

If you need a date night restaurant or a place to impress your in-laws, **La Meilleure Jeunesse** is just that!

The décor is eclectic - plush velvet couches in the entrance (reminiscent of a Parisian boudoir) lead to the restaurant, filled with white linen table tops & silver candle stick holders, overlooking the cutest little terrace, making you forget you are just off Avenue Louise! It is elegance personified!

Start with a cocktail (I recommend the Gin Cucumber) and peruse the menu. Be sure you come hungry, as this is definitely a starter, main course, and dessert kind of place.

Food is served with flair. Take the starter of '*Tartare de Dorade a la Japonaise*' and a glass of smoke will be elegantly whipped off your plate at your table, to present the fish tartare. Everything else served thereafter will also have you smiling – not just in presentation but also in taste!

It isn't cheap but it definitely has the wow factor! <u>La Meilleure Jeunesse</u> - 58 Rue de L'Aurore

Beaucoup Fish

From **Amy Choin** - Blogs in English, at <u>Bela Lumo</u>

Brussels has an abundance of seafood restaurants, but in my opinion, newcomer **Beaucoup Fish** stands way out from the crowd. Their menu changes regularly, according to what's available at the market, and they truly do use only the freshest ingredients. They offer a good selection of original dishes, while still offering many of the Belgian classics like shrimp croquettes and moules frites. If you like your seafood drowning in heavy sauces, this is not the place for you. The chef lets the seafood be the star here. You may be tempted to skip dessert after your meal, but in this case, I would urge you to find some room. The desserts have been given just as much thought as the rest of the menu. They're big enough to share, though you won't want to once you have a taste!

The service is top notch, with a multilingual and friendly staff. They strike just the right balance between familiar and formal, and the small number of tables means you're in for a personal and intimate dining experience. As if it couldn't get any more perfect, the restaurant itself is gorgeous. The minimalist and modern design features wood and marble, but the best part are the many subtle fishy details.

While the location near the Royal Flemish Theater is a little rough around the edges, don't be put off. It only adds to the feeling that you've just discovered Brussels' best-kept secret. <u>Beaucoup Fish</u> - Rue Van Gaverstraat 2

Notos

From **Françoise Vangelder** - Blogs in French, at <u>La Cuisine de Françoise</u>

Food is all about sensation, isn't it?

When I entered **Notos** Restaurant, I enjoyed the same feeling I experienced years ago on Santorini island, sitting at the terrace of a typical tiny Greek restaurant, where I had the most amazing stuffed cabbage of my life!

Notos offers a diverse and refined cuisine. The Chef proposes a menu where each dish is prepared with a limited number of ingredients, in order to respect the quality, and mainly organic, products he imports directly from Greece. He could tell you the story of the products, as well as the names of all the producers. The time he spends selecting these ingredients is part of his secret.

The Chef prepared each dish on the menu, putting the highlight on very authentic and simple products, while at the same time giving them a modern touch. Modernity meets with tradition and simplicity in each plate.

I would highly recommend this very good address to all refined food lovers who would like to enjoy a nice and relaxed lunch or dinner!

Notos - 154 Rue de Livourne

Menma

From **Giusi Genduso** - Blogs in French, at Healthy Living

Menma is a ramen noodle bar and 'must visit' if you appreciate traditional Japanese food. What makes the restaurant special is the majority of the ingredients are homemade or come from local farms. For example, the noodles are made by hand and the pork is from Belgium. It is always pleasant to dine at a restaurant with these kind of values!

The luckiest clients will have the opportunity to watch the preparation of their ramen bowl at the bar... It is worth the detour and it is always fascinating.

The staff is very professional and polite. The prices are fair for the quality on the plate. You should expect 12-15€ for one bowl of ramen noodles.

Menma is based on simplicity. This is why the restaurant features a minimalist menu, with a small number of starters and/or ramen bowls. Don't expect a 10-page menu at Menma.The drinks menu is also interesting, because Menma promotes the Belgian-Japanese collaboration on the creation of beers. Don't be afraid to let yourself go for a foreign beer just for the evening!

For our vegan and vegetarian friends, it is possible to customize your ramen bowl, by choosing supplements of veggies or seaweeds.

Menma restaurant is a simple and refined place that's worth a look! Oh, did you know the word 'Menma' means Chinese bamboo? Menma - Avenue des Saisons 123

San

From **Gregory Bogaert** - Blogs in French, at Cook & Roll

Sang-Hoon Degeimbre and Toshiro Fujii have brought the best products, expertise, techniques, and associations, developed for years in **San**'s double starred restaurant, to Brussels. Dishes are constructed as bowls, in which a few carefully chosen elements are cooked, combined, and meant to be eaten with a spoon. The contrasts in complementary colours, textures, temperatures, crunchiness, and tastes, makes each spoonful a delight for the palate.

San's cuisine is a perfect mix of the latest cooking techniques applied to the best produce from the Belgian "terroir", including a wide variety of carefully grown vegetables, plants, and herbs from its own garden in Liernu. The restaurant is beautifully decorated in yellow and light blue shades and can accommodate about 30 seats.

However, I would highly recommend sitting at the bar along the kitchen on the ground floor, to admire the precision and skills of the chefs creating your bowls, while you get to enjoy eating them! <u>San</u> - Rue de Flandre 19

Izakaya

From **Emmanuelle Hubert** - Blogs in French, at <u>Au Goût d'Emma</u>

Looking for an authentic Japanese meal in Brussels? Then **Izakaya**, located near Avenue Louise in Ixelles, is the perfect place to go. This small restaurant is always full of both Japanese expats and Brussels locals, which is always a good sign! Book ahead and choose a seat at the bar, to watch the Sushi Master at work. Many say his sashimis are the best in Brussels – my personal favourite is the cold octopus salad. If you don't enjoy raw food, try one of Izakaya's skewers, with their "special" sauce. For dessert, be sure not miss their matcha tea ice cream. **Izakaya** - Chaussée de Vleurgat 123

TAN

From **Sandy T.** - Blogs in English, at <u>S Marks The Spots</u>

Brussels offers abundant choice, when it comes to indulgent food, so when you blog about great foodie spots in the city, it becomes hard to maintain a healthy diet. Luckily, one of my all-time favourite restaurants strikes the balance between healthy and delicious!

TAN is located in Châtelain, one of the most beautiful and lively areas in Brussels. The ground floor hosts a grocery shop where you can find a good variety of organic and bio foodie products that are also used in the restaurant on the first floor.

As is often the case in Brussels, you need to know where to look, in order to discover the hidden gems. Follow the stairway, at the back of the store to the first floor, and you are in for a treat. The modern, white interior, set up according to the principles of feng shui, will definitely surprise you in the most positive way. I also love the little terrace, which is wonderful for an al fresco meal on a sunny day.

TAN serves living food, which means the ingredients are prepared at low temperatures or retained raw, to preserve all their nutritional value that would otherwise be destroyed by cooking. The menu changes regularly, depending on the season, and all dishes are beautifully presented and taste incredibly good – you cannot go wrong no matter what you choose.

If you are a vegetarian, have dietary restrictions, or are simply looking for a restaurant with interesting food combinations, put TAN on your list. Make sure to reserve in advance and enjoy! TAN - Rue de l'Aqueduc 95

Kocharata

From **Marion Bonduelle** - Blogs in French, at <u>Crumbles et Cassonade</u>

Not being able to travel as much as I would like, I enjoy discovering restaurants that allow me travel through different cuisines - and there are plenty to choose from in Saint-Gilles! Among the Portuguese, Ecuadorian, Greek, Chilean, Italian, Iranian and Peruvian restaurants, near 'la barrière,' we find **Kocharata**, a restaurant that takes us straight to Bulgaria!

The exterior, with its dark façade and heavy wooden door, isn't enticing. But don't let appearances fool you. Behind the austere frontage hides a warm and traditional place that transports you from the capital of Europe, with seats trimmed with embroidered cushions, dark wood, red tablecloths, and garlic and chili braids. It doesn't hurt that the owner is very sweet.

The food is simple and tasty, with Greek and Turkish influences. The menu is varied, and showcases cheese and grilled meat dishes. As a starter, I succumbed to the cheese grilled as they do in the mountains: a dish garnished with sheep cheese, egg, tomatoes and spices, flambeed, so the cheese is perfectly melted before serving. Or you can flame grill your own brochettes, on small individual spits, at the table. A warm atmosphere is guaranteed! Don't miss trying Kocharata's own 'bear wine'!

It is impossible not to end this culinary voyage to Bulgaria with a pancake topped with a delicious rose jam.

Kocharata is open for lunch and every evening except Sunday. Kocharata - Avenue du Parc 4

Hong Kong Delight

From **Apolina Fos** - Blogs in English and French at Bombay-Bruxelles

When asked to choose a great restaurant in Brussels, I immediately thought of **Hong Kong Delight**. This little place is in the middle of Brussels' tiny China Town and bang in the city centre. The first time I visited, it was quite by accident. Looking for a quick bite before catching a movie, we found the first place that was open. The Hong Kong delight is not a big restaurant. But what struck us was at least half of the patrons were of Chinese descent.

We took our seats at our modest table... this place is not about designer furniture or about posh interiors. You'll find the best part on your plate! The menu is quite extensive, but there are some pearls there. This is the only place in Brussels (and probably in Belgium) where you will find unusual dishes like duck's tongues deep fried with spices and salt, fried chicken blood with ginger, crispy pork intestine, steamed chicken feet in black beans, tofu with pidan (1000 year eggs) and jelly fish with cucumber.

But don't you worry; there are the usual dim-sums, wantons and other soups, as well as the typical stir-fries. One of the specialities is Peking Duck, which is one of the most popular dishes on the menu.

Cost-wise, Hong Kong Delight is one of the most reasonably priced restaurants in the European Capital. Starters are 4-10€ and mains start at 10€. The service is no-nonsense and efficient.

This is a place I like to visit often, for a surprising and satisfying meal. **Hong Kong Delight** - Rue Sainte Catherine 35

Where NOT to Eat

Being a full-time traveller myself, I understand, sometimes there isn't time to consult a guidebook or make reservations ahead - you just need to eat something. Now.

Food is never far from hand in Brussels, but it's not always something worth spending your hard-earned cash on. And as a foodie Mecca, you should **never** have to suffer through a bad meal in Brussels. So, in a pinch, to avoid a case of the hangries, here are a few of my top tips on where **not** to eat in Brussels.

Rule #1 - If you ignore everything else in this guide, please (please) do not eat on Rue des Bouchers. Yes it's close to Grand Place. Yes it's quaint and picturesque. And yes, there are plenty of restaurants to choose from. But trust me on this; they are, at best, overpriced and lacking in quality and, at worst, a case of food-poisoning waiting to happen. These restaurants prey on tourists, with menus in multiple languages and bright colour photos, and men whose sole job is to drag unsuspecting tourists inside for overpriced seafood dinners. With great seafood just steps away on Place Sainte Catherine, there is no need to eat here. Ever.

Rule #2 - No good restaurant in Brussels needs to hire someone to attract diners. If someone is trying to entice you to eat somewhere (like Rue des Bouchers) just move along.

Rule #3 - Menus in multiple languages are *de rigueur* in Brussels. However, those languages should be French and Flemish (Dutch) and, increasingly English. If a menu sports 11 languages and colourful flags of the world, it caters to tourists and you don't want to eat there.

Rule #4 - When in doubt, go where the locals go. Bruxellois tend to eat late (It's tough to get a meal before 7pm). If you walk into a restaurant at 8pm and it's empty, chances are, there's a reason for that. Conversely, if a restaurant is humming, and the majority of folks are speaking French, it's likely a safe bet.

Rule #5 - Whenever possible, plan ahead. I understand the desire for spontaneity, but why risk disappointment? If you've spotted a restaurant in this guide, you really want to try, make reservations. It

116

will save on regret and tragic bad food experiences, no foodie should have to suffer through, especially not in Brussels.

Belgian Restaurant Etiquette

If you've never eaten out in Belgium before, there are a few restaurant customs that may seem a bit strange to outsiders. When travelling, I like to know the basic etiquette of the country I'm visiting so I don't make a total fool of myself.

To avoid some common tourist gaffs, here are a few notes on Belgian restaurant etiquette to keep in mind when dining out.

- Belgians typically dress up to go out although it is more casual than it once was. These days, even the Michelin-starred restaurants don't require a jacket and tie or a fancy dress. However, in fine-dining restaurants you'll want to put in a bit of effort. Avoid jeans, shorts, t-shits, and the like.

- Never order coffee at the start of your meal. Belgians only take their hot drinks as an end to the meal. If you order coffee first, your server will assume you aren't ordering food and coffee is all you will get.

- Dining, especially at dinnertime, is a drawn out affair of at least 3 courses. Expect your meal to last much longer than it would in North America. Sit back, relax, and enjoy the company and food, as a Belgian would.

- In Belgium it is considered rude for the server to bring your check before you ask for it. When you are finished your meal and are ready to leave, simply signal to the waiter and ask for your bill.

- Service fees are typically added to the bill in Belgium and restaurant staff is paid fair wages. While tipping isn't required and not all Belgians tip, 5-10% to your server is customary. For small bills, just round up to the nearest euro.

- With the exception of some Asian and other international restaurants, getting a 'doggie bag' isn't customary in Belgium. Many restaurants won't have take away containers, so don't order extra assuming you can take it with you.

A Quick Guide to Restaurant Prices

I haven't included prices for most of the restaurants listed in the guide simply because prices fluctuate regularly. However, I do want to give you a few rough guidelines, so you can budget appropriately.

- For a typical Belgian breakfast of coffee and a pastry expect to pay €5-7

- For a quick lunch of 1-2 courses (without alcohol) expect to pay €20-30
- For dinner at one of the 'Cheap Eats' restaurants listed budget €20-30
- For a cocktail at a bar budget €12-15
- For a draft beer or glass of house wine at a café budget €5-8

Average prices at a fine-dining or brasserie style restaurant:
- starters: €8-16
- mains: €18-26
- wines: €25-50
- 3-course set menu: €35-55

For Michelin quality restaurants expect:
- starters: €25-45
- mains: €28-60
- wines: from €45
- menu: €60-150

WHAT TO DO BETWEEN MEALS

Brussels has endless possibilities for things to do, from countless museums, to beautiful green-spaces, to the EU institutions, and stunning Art Nouveau architecture.

However, for the purposes of this guide, we're focusing, specifically, on the best activities for foodies. With a variety of great food and drink festivals, cooking classes and food tours, and even food-themed museums, there's plenty to keep foodies in Brussels entertained between meals.

Bookalokal

One thing I recommend to all visitors to Brussels, foodies or not, is to attend a **Bookalokal** event. This is not only a great way to enjoy a budget-friendly meal, but also to meet local people who are passionate and knowledgeable about their city. It's a great opportunity for foodies to pick the brains of their hosts about local secrets - from where to eat, to the best place to buy ingredients for sushi (See Tagawa Market in the International Ingredients section below).

The Bookalokal concept is simple. A host signs up to offer a food experience, and guests sign up and pay for a food experience of their choice. The experiences can be sit-down meals, beer or wine tastings, cooking classes, food and art events, or anything else involving food. I even attended a Murder Mystery dinner.

Bookalokal was started by an American expat in Brussels, and she has since expanded her website to cover events around the world. It's a brilliant concept and it's become extremely popular in the Brussels expat community. People looking to share good food from their home countries are filling missing niches in the international restaurant scene. I've been particularly impressed by the Indian offerings.

Sign up for Bookalokal using this referral code and you'll get 10$ off your first event.

Food Tours

The second thing I recommend, to all visitors in Brussels, is to book a tour with the Brussels Greeters. When it comes to guided tours, you often get what you pay for. Luckily, this is not the case with the Brussels Greeters. This talented, passionate group of volunteers is ready to show you every nook and cranny of the city, absolutely free.

The Brussels Greeters are part of the International Greeter network and are made up of volunteers from all walks of life. Many are locals, born and bred in Brussels. Some are expats, passionate about their adopted home. They are historians, architects, designers, foodies, and art-lovers, which means you can take a tour with the theme of your choice.

A Brussels Greeters tour can give you a great overview of Brussels' highlights, if it's your first visit. However, there are new sights to be seen, even if you consider yourself a Brussels expert. After living in, and writing about, Brussels for 8 years, I consider myself 'in the know.' I requested a Greeter show me a neighbourhood I hadn't spent much time in and was fascinated by everything I learned. We also had a great discussion about urban planning, expat life, and design in Belgium.

Foodies can request tours of Brussels top culinary destinations, or you can focus your efforts on a particular food, like chocolate.

The Brussels Greeters should be your first stop when you arrive in Brussels (or, better yet, email them before you arrive, because their services are very much in demand). The heart of Brussels is in its neighbourhoods and its citizens. The Brussels Greeters offer you both, for free. (Read an extended article on my tour with the Brussels Greeters)

Other food tour options are also available, for a fee, through **Bookalokal** (see above). We enjoyed an excellent beer tour of Brussels and discovered a few new cafés from our local guide.

Museums for Foodies

There are over 100 museums in Brussels and many of them are worth your time and attention. However, there are a few museums of particular interest to foodies you should definitely add to your agenda.

Cantillon Brewery

No trip to Belgium is complete without experiencing the Belgian beer culture. The best place in Brussels to take a look at beer history is the **Cantillon Brewery**. Even as a non-beer-drinker, it's a fascinating place to visit.

One of the things that makes Cantillon so special is it has hardly changed, since it opened its doors in 1900, (including the dust and cobwebs!) The second unique aspect of Cantillon is the spontaneous fermentation of its tart Lambic beers, which only happens in this tiny area of Belgium. Beer really is in the air around Brussels!

Cantillon beers are 100% organic and come in a variety of styles and flavours, from traditional Lambic and Faro beer, to the tart cherry beer, Kriek.

Tours take place every day, in multiple languages, and if you're lucky your visit could coincide with brewing or bottling days. Cantillon Brewery - Rue Gheude 56 (Read Andrew's extended article on Lambic Beer and Cantillon Brewery)

Schaerbeek Beer Museum

True Belgian beer lovers should check out the bite-sized **Museum of Belgian Beer**, in Schaerbeek. In addition to brewing paraphernalia, the museum has over 1000 bottles and glasses from just about every beer brewed in the country (and some that no longer exist.)

Another great reason to visit - the museum has its own beer, only available at the on-site café. Staff are passionate about the collection, so don't be afraid to ask questions. Schaerbeek Museum of Beer - Avenue Louis Bertrand 33-35

Belgian Chocolate Village

Although it's a bit of a trek to get there, the **Belgian Chocolate Village**, in the Koekelberg neighbourhood, is worth the effort for choco-holics.

One of the newest museums in Brussels, the Belgian Chocolate Village tells the story of chocolate, from bean to praline, with audio-guides available in seven languages.

One unique feature is the museum's greenhouse replicating the exact conditions necessary to grow cacao beans.

Of course, the main reason to visit is the museum's tasting room, offering chocolates from artisan *chocolatiers* from around Belgium, for sale as edible souvenirs.

Serious chocolate-lovers can attend one of the museum's workshops, hosted by local chocolate makers; a deliciously educational experience. <u>Belgian Chocolate Village</u> - Rue de Neck 20

Cooking Classes

There's no better way to understand a culture than by understanding its food. While eating and enjoying a cuisine is a great way to do this, learning to cook it yourself brings even more depth to the experience.

Luckily, in Brussels, there's plenty of opportunity to do just that. With cooking classes in traditional Belgian cuisine, pasta making, and world food cookery, you can find a class in just about every type of food you can imagine.

A great place to start is **Bookalokal** (See Foodie Must Dos above), where you can learn to cook in the home of a passionate local foodie. The classes change often and every type of cooking class, from Belgian food to South American cuisine, has been up for grabs.

Mains à la Pâte

<u>Mains à la Pâte</u> is the brainchild of Chef Michele Ambrosio, a friendly, young, Italian expat in Brussels. The concept behind Michele's project is elegantly simple – sharing Italian culture and tradition through the making of fresh pasta.

Mains à la Pâte is more than just a cooking class where you follow step-by-step instructions, although this is an important aspect. While learning how, you also learn why. As you get stuck in kneading pasta dough, Michele shares some of the traditions, legends, songs, and even poetry surrounding the pasta. Who knew there was so much to say about tagliatelle!

Another great reason to love Mains à la Pâte is Michele's commitment to sustainability. He endeavours to use locally sourced, organic products wherever possible. In the few cases there is no good local alternative, he uses organic products straight from Italy.

Classes are available in English, French, and Italian. Prices range from 30€-60€ per person for groups of 3-10 people (including the class, a full meal, and take home recipes and information.)

Laurent Gerbaud Chocolate Workshops

Nothing could be more decadent than getting your hands into Belgian chocolate and while you're indulging, why not learn a valuable skill too? Master *chocolatier*, Laurent Gerbaud, offers the opportunity to do just that at his chocolate making workshops.

You'll learn how to make chocolate treats and how to blend chocolate from different beans to create unique flavours, in this hands-on class. Of course, there's plenty of taste-testing too.

Be sure to book ahead as these free classes are extremely popular.

Laurent Gerbaud - Rue Ravenstein 2D

Mmmmh!

If you ask anyone in Brussels about cooking classes, no doubt **Mmmmh!** will come up, so I'd be remiss if I didn't mention it here. Without a doubt, they offer the widest selection of cooking classes in the city. Currently, Mmmmh!'s agenda includes everything from Thai to English cuisine and everything in between.

I'll admit, I haven't attended a class at Mmmmh! in years and, when I did, it was with mixed results. One class I attended was very hands on and well worth the fee paid. Another I tried was a cooking demo only, the class was huge, and I didn't feel I took anything practical away from it.

Mmmmh!'s classes are also primarily in French, however this can be a fun and less intimidating way to practise your language skills. My advice would be to read the course description very carefully and ask any questions you might have, before signing up. That said, Mmmmh!'s cooking space is beautiful, there are classes scheduled throughout the day, with even quickie 'lunch break' classes, and the prices vary to suit all budgets. Mmmmh! - Chaussée de Charleroi 92

Food Festivals

Any time of year is a great time to visit Brussels, if you're a foodie. However, it can be a great opportunity to time your visit to coincide with one of the capital's top food and drink events. There are festivals featuring Brussels' Michelin-starred chefs, top food trucks, world wines, and, of course, Belgian beer. Choose your event from my favourites below.

EAT! Brussels

If you want to plan your visit to Brussels around one food festival, EAT! Brussels should be the one. This food festival is a weekend-long celebration of the city's restaurants, bars, and caterers, in one of Brussels' lovely parks, normally in early October. It's a great way to sample the cuisines of more than 25 Brussels restaurants, without the risk or expense of booking a table for an entire meal.

Visitors purchase bags of tokens that can be exchanged for food or drink at any of the stalls. The restaurants range from neighbourhood favourites to Michelin-starred fine dining. I've discovered some great new restaurants at past events.

In addition to Brussels-based cuisine, there are always a number of regions from elsewhere in Europe, and around the world. Past events have included food from various regions of China, Congo, Morocco, Bulgaria, Slovenia, Canada and Poland.

There are also classes and events throughout the weekend such as wine tasting and pairing, cocktail making, and cooking classes.

Brussels Food Truck Festival

The Brussels Food Truck Festival began in 2014 and, with the current food-truck craze, there is huge potential for this festival to grow. Food Trucks are quickly popping up around the city, but without one fixed place for them to set up, it's difficult to discover new ones. At the Food Truck Festival, in early May, you can taste-test your way through more than 30 trucks from around Belgium, the Netherlands, France, and Luxembourg. (For more on the food truck craze, read my article on the Top Food Trucks in Belgium)

Culinaria

Like EAT! Brussels, Culinaria is a festival for Belgian chefs to show their stuff. Not limited to Brussels, it attracts the top chefs from around the country, many of them sporting a Michelin Star or two (or three!). The standard of the food is extremely high (especially considering the volume of dishes produced) and the cuisine is innovative. Over the past years, Culinaria has grown to add classes, display cooking, and other foodie mini-events. It has also grown beyond Brussels and now hosts events at the Belgian coast.

In all honesty, I have mixed feelings about Culinaria. The first year, I loved it. I attended the second year and, although it was larger and the food was excellent, it was disorganised and I left with mixed feelings. The third year I attended, I was disappointed. The service just wasn't there: Reception was frosty; several of the restaurants ran out of food well before the end of the event and I just generally felt I didn't get my money's worth. That said, the event has tremendous potential and I know many folks who love it still. I'm willing to give it another chance, in the future, and I hope the service related kinks are worked out for future events, as it's a great opportunity to see Belgium's finest chefs under one roof. Culinaria takes place in multiple locations around Brussels, and Belgium, at various times of the year. Check their website for the next edition.

Dinner in the Sky

Who doesn't want to eat an incredible meal prepared right in front of you by a Michelin-starred chef in a location with a gorgeous view. Every summer in Brussels, you can do just that – dangling from a crane suspended over the Brussels skyline, with Dinner in the Sky.

This isn't a festival exactly and, when I participated, it was supposed to be a one-time event. But, like the Tram Experience, it was so popular it was made an annual event. The experience is incredible, even for someone as scared of heights as me.

The Dinner in the Sky 'restaurant' is essentially a mini kitchen surrounded by a counter and 22 seats. Up to five people can work in the centre kitchen area, while diners are strapped into the chairs with harnesses, around the outside. The seats pivot from side to side, so you can turn partway around to admire the view behind you.

It also gives you the once-in-a-lifetime chance to be face to face with a Michelin-starred chef; for me it was Luigi Ciciriello, the master behind La Truffe Noire.

This once-in-a-lifetime chance does come with a price tag to match. However, if the weather-gods are favourable, it's worth the splurge for an unforgettable meal. (Read <u>my extended review of Dinner in the Sky</u>)

Megavino

We can't have food without wine and Brussels is home to the biggest wine festival in Benelux. <u>Megavino,</u> in late October at the Brussels Expo, is host to over 360 wine exhibitors from around the world, organised by region. Of course, you can find plenty of your favourite French, Spanish, and Italian wines, but you can also taste wines from some lesser-known regions. I was thrilled to discover Bulgarian wine and the wines I tried from Uruguay were excellent. I also tried many Belgian wines that pleasantly surprised me.

For the cost of admission (normally around €10), you receive a tasting glass and a catalogue of available wines (so you can be sure to track your favourites). Of course, being in Belgium, those wines need to be paired with great foods too and you'll find a variety of gourmet delicacies to take away and eat on-site.

Belgian Beer Weekend

Beer culture is essential in Belgium and there's nowhere you can see more of the history and tradition around Belgian Beer than the Belgian Beer Weekend, held every September, in Brussels. Of course, there's plenty of beer drinking, but the festival celebrates more than just beer appreciation.

You can experience the 'benediction of the beer' as it is blessed in a church in honour of the patron Saint of brewers, Saint Arnould. There are historic processions, seminars, and plenty of music.

The beer tents on Grand Place host almost 50 brewers, from giants like AB INBEV and Palm, to small organic brewers like Caracole. Many of the authentic Trappist breweries attend the event, as well.

Winter Wonders Christmas Market

Despite the typically dreary weather in December, the Christmas season is a great time for foodies to visit Brussels. The Brussels Christmas Market, <u>Winter Wonders,</u> is much more than food, but honestly the food is the best part.

Discover the special guest regions and sample some delicacies from abroad. Or choose traditional favourites like glühwein (hot, spiced red wine) and sausages. I always try to track down a tartiflette (a French dish of potatoes, cheese, and bacon). You can also shop for goodies to stock your cupboards from the many producers selling their wares in the little wooden chalets. You can find everything from foie gras from southwest France, to Canadian maple products. Yum!

All year, my husband and I look forward to our annual tradition of Champagne, oysters, and foie gras, under the twinkling light display on the Grand Place. There's no more magical way to celebrate the holidays. (Read <u>my extended article on Brussels Winter Wonders</u>)

SHOPPING FOR FOODIES

All of the foodies I know love to shop for cooking supplies, almost as much as they love to eat (myself included!). Whether it's the latest kitchen gadget or gourmet ingredients for your next meal, this section will give you all the secrets for the best foodie shopping in Brussels.

Markets

Of course, we can't discuss foodie shopping, without mentioning the vibrant street markets.

Every neighbourhood in Brussels has its own market at least once a week. They vary in size but most have a mix of local produce, baked goods, cheap clothing, and household goods. All of the street markets have at least a couple of street food options, usually sausages, seafood and, of course, the inevitable Belgian French fry.

Flagey

The foodie offerings at the **Place Flagey market** are better than most. There are beautiful homemade pastas, fresh honey, local cheeses, and even tasty take-away Asian food. For on-site dining, favourite food-truck **Keep on Toasting** often makes an appearance, with its upscale toasted sandwiches.

With the vibrant veggies, marvellous meats and delectable desserts it's impossible to leave empty handed. **Place Eugène Flagey** (Saturday and Sunday from 7am - 2:30pm)

Midi Market

For sheer size, the **market at Brussels South train station** (Gare du Midi) takes the prize. Here you'll find plenty of produce vendors, spices, olives, nuts, and even some kitchenware.

There are some good deals to be found here, particularly an hour before closing. But be warned, this market can be packed and it's a prime target for pickpockets, so be aware of your belongings at all times. **Brussels South Station** (Sunday 8am - 1pm)

Cooking Supplies

If you just can't live without the latest kitchen gadget, there are a few great places to visit in Brussels.

The shop at **Mmmmh!** (mentioned in the Cooking Classes section above) has an excellent (albeit pricey) selection of cookware and cookbooks, as well as some gourmet ingredients.

International Home of Cooking

Cooks and foodies shouldn't miss the **International Home of Cooking**. They stock every gadget and gizmo you've ever wanted for your kitchen (and some you didn't even know you wanted). You can find everything from high-quality chef's knives to small appliances, baking supplies, and a vast array of cookbooks (although most are in French or Dutch).

There are goodies for foodies too (cupcake workshop anyone?). Choose from two locations - one on the prestigious Avenue Louise and the other just steps from the Galeries Royale, near Grand Place. The shops often have live demos of appliances and cooking techniques, so you can pick up some handy tips and tricks while you shop. International Home of Cooking - Rue Léopold 3

Dille & Kamille

For inexpensive but lovely housewares and kitchen gadgets, don't miss the Dutch chain, Dille & Kamille. In addition to affordable tableware, the shop stocks loose teas, handmade soaps and candles, candies, linens, and fresh herbs. Dille & Kamille - Rue Jean Stas 16

Gourmet Shopping

There's no better souvenir than an edible souvenir (especially as you won't have to dust it later). The following shops stock great gourmet gifts for foodies, both from Belgium and beyond.

Maison Dandoy

Maison Dandoy is a Belgian institution and they have been making cookies in Brussels, since 1829. The cookies are from 100% natural ingredients and some of the recipes are 180 years old. The tearoom is also home to the best waffle in Brussels, for my money. (Read more in the 'Belgian Foods' section above)

Try the traditional Belgian speculoos, a spicy biscuit a bit like gingerbread, or Pain a la Greque, a Brussels favourite. There is even an Earl Grey cookie with tealeaves – delicious.

Not only do Dandoy cookies taste wonderful, but their packaging is lovely, making them the perfect gift. Choose from the newly designed Maison Dandoy boxes or a variety of tin boxes, perfect for travelling.

<u>Maison Dandoy</u> has numerous locations around Brussels, including Sablon and steps from Grand Place.

Pappabubble

Hard candies may seem old-fashioned but the tiny **Pappabubble** shop, near Grand Place, is bringing these traditional sweets to a new, modern level. The candies are hand-made in the shop, using all-natural ingredients. There are no E numbers here, as all of the vibrant colours come from plants. The 30+ flavours range from traditional favourites like lemon and strawberry, to coconut cream and mojito (a favourite!).

If you're lucky, the candy-makers will be hard at work, pulling huge tubes of candy by hand. It's fascinating to watch the designs appear before your eyes. Pappabubble even creates custom candies with corporate logos or special messages. <u>Pappabubble</u> ▪ Rue du Marché au Charbon, 13

Champigros

If you're searching for the best gourmet offerings from Europe's forests and fields, don't miss the **Champigros** shop, near Place Sainte Catherine. The shop's name comes from a combination of the French words "champignons grossiste," or mushroom wholesaler. If you are a friend of the fungus, this is your shop. Step inside to discover the best truffles, morelles, girolles, chanterelles and more.

Even if you aren't a mushroom fanatic, there are still foodie delights to tempt you. Champigros also sells beautiful fresh produce and delicatessen treats that are easier to pack in your suitcase than a kilo of Cêpes. The shop is fantastic year round but it is particularly wonderful in autumn when the majority of the wild forest mushrooms are in their peak season. Champigros - Rue Sainte-Catherine 36

Le Fraysse

For years, I lamented the lack of a one-stop shop, in Brussels, where you could buy all of the wonderful artisanal products from small, local producers around Belgium. Recently, I discovered **Le Fraysse** and it is the exact shop I had been dreaming of.

Le Fraysse is a bio-organic shop, featuring wonderful artisanal products hand-selected by the owners, from around Belgium and the neighbouring countries. There are cheeses, sausages, jams, sweets, cookies, breads, and even foie-gras.

144

There is also a variety of sustainable household products, like soaps and shampoos, cleaning products, and personal care items. But my favourite part of the shop (I like to refer to as the wall of goodness) is the beverages wall. Here you can find the best Belgian drinks, from juice to wine and liqueurs, and, of course, a variety of Belgian beer. It's a great shop if you're looking for a hostess gift or a special treat all for yourself. <u>Le Fraysse</u> - Chaussée de Louvain 896 (Read <u>my extended article on Le Fraysse</u>)

Rob

Brussels' largest gourmet supermarket, Rob, is well worth the trip outside the city centre, for dedicated foodies. This market is filled with all of the finest grocery items from around Europe. This is where locals go to buy hard-to-find ingredients and where expats go to find their favourite tastes of home.

There are vast meat, seafood, cheese, and deli counters and the bakery is a pastry-lover's dream. Rob stocks chocolate from all of Brussels' top chocolatiers, for the ultimate in one-stop Belgian chocolate shopping.

The wine selection here is beyond compare. Everyday wines and spirits can be found in the main shop but if you're looking for something really special, descend into the basement. Here, you will find a dedicated wine cellar, with sommeliers on hand to help you choose the perfect bottle. If your tastes run to high-end whiskeys, vodkas, cognacs, and the like, there is also a dedicated shop just for you. It's kept under lock and key and if you have to ask the prices, it's best to move along.

Visit on a Saturday when the shop demonstrators are active and you can taste your way around Europe. <u>Rob</u> - Boulevard de la Woluwe 28, 1150 Woluwe-Saint-Pierre

International Ingredients

Whether you live in Brussels or are just visiting, it can be fun (and educational) to visit some of the vast array of international food shops in the city. It would take an entire book to list all of them, so I've just singled out a few of the biggest and best. However, you can find a full listing by cuisine in this <u>list of International food stores in Brussels</u>.

Kam-Yuen

If you love all things Asian, don't miss the quirky, chaotic **Kam-Yuen Supermarket**, near Place Sainte Catherine. Duck under the giant purple and green KY sign (trying not to snicker at the unfortunate initials) and dive into the most random shop in the city. The 'organisation' of the store is mind-boggling but I'm sure in someone's mind it made sense to put the 'American' peanut butter beside the deep fried crispy anchovies.

It is truly Asian in the sense that you can find foods from China, Japan, India, Indonesia, Vietnam, England, and the US (apparently these last two have changed continents since I last looked at a map). It's also much larger than it seems from the outside, with aisle after aisle of unusual ingredients. Don't expect any help finding what you need (unless you speak Mandarin) and friendly service is usually out of the question. But you can expect to find something different and tasty on every visit. <u>Kam-Yuen Supermarket</u> - Rue de la Vierge Noir 2-4

Jack O'Shea's

If you love to BBQ, or are just a fan of a really great steak, **Jack O'Shea's** butcher shop, in the EU Quarter, is like a candy-shop for carnivores. This is the Brussels location of the famous London butcher and it's a one-stop shop for the best quality meats in the city.

Jack's hand-made sausages come in a dozen varieties and the seasonal game meats are as fresh as can be. They even carry the world famous Wagyu beef.

But even vegetarians have plenty of reasons to visit Jack's. For starters, they have a fantastic new world wine selection and their British and local cheeses are mouth-watering. You can also stock up on plenty of imported grocery items from sauces, to crisps, to German beer. Don't miss the brownies in the deli case – chocolate heaven! Jack O'Shea's - Rue Le Titien 30

MexiGo

Although small, **MexiGo** is a treasure trove of Mexican ingredients

– dried peppers, sauces, dried beans and cans of re-fried beans, nacho chips, tequila, homemade tortillas, and enough hot sauce to start a house fire.

There's also an odd mix of American foods: Jello, a variety of cereals, Pop-Tarts, Hamburger Helper, and Betty Crocker and Aunt Jemima. Don't miss the take-away burritos! (See the 'International Cuisine' section above) MexiGo - 47 Francois Dons

Ideal Cash & Carry

If I could only shop at one store in this list, **Ideal Cash & Carry Indian & Pakistani foods** would be the one. The store isn't huge, but it is jam packed with good things – many of which you don't have to be into Indian cuisine to appreciate. It's worth the trip just to buy spices alone. You can stock up on 250g bags (or much larger) for little more than a euro, as opposed to those tiny jars you get at the supermarket for three euro or more.

The quantity of basmati rice is staggering and the cost is a fraction of what you will pay at Belgian supermarkets. Cash and Carry also stocks nuts at great prices. For people on gluten-free diets, Cash and Carry offers rice and gram flour which make good wheat replacements.

As for Indian ingredients, there is a large selection of pre-made curry pastes, like Patak's, a small selection of fresh chilli peppers and

150

other Indian produce, some pre-made Indian meals, a small frozen section with great samosas, and some Indian dairy products like paneer cheese. Ideal Cash and Carry - Chaussée de Gand, 33 (Read my extended review of Ideal Cash & Carry)

Tagawa

Tagawa is a firm favourite with Japanese expats and anyone who loves eating and making sushi. It's a hidden away two-storey shop, filled with Japanese goodies. The ground floor has freshly made sushi and other items to take-away. There are also several freezers filled with ingredients and pre-made items like dumplings and steamed buns. There is also a fish counter selling sushi-grade fish, so you can roll your own at home.

Upstairs is a dizzying array of noodles and sweets, as well as sauces, alcohol, and small selection of dishes and kitchen items, and Japanese books and magazines. If you're looking for hard-to-find Japanese ingredients, it's likely you'll find them at Tagawa. Tagawa Japanese Shop - Chaussée de Vleurgat, 119

Stonemanor

Although it's not actually in Brussels, **Stonemanor** is close enough and big enough to be a firm favourite with expats from all over Belgium. The original Everberg location was my lifesaver when I first moved to Belgium, especially since it was just down the street from my old home.

With three stories packed with food, drinks, English magazines, books, cards and more, it really is a little oasis of all things Anglo. Stonemanor also allows you to order from UK shops like Waitrose, John Lewis, and Argos, and they've recently opened a tearoom – fresh scones anyone? Stock up on British cheeses, fresh baked samosas, and tea... lots of tea. Stonemanor also carries a good variety of Gluten-free products for folks with dietary issues. Stonemanor - Steenhofstraat 28, Everberg

Wine, Beer & Spirits

Beer, wine, and spirits are widely available in grocery stores in Belgium. However, if you are looking for something special, local, or just want some good advice, it's well worth seeking out a speciality liquor shop. In this section, you'll find my favourites.

Buying Belgian Beer

Buying Belgian beer in Brussels is as easy as popping into the corner store. Although you won't typically find a huge selection at the local grocery store, they will usually carry a small mix of brands and varieties.

Many grocery stores stock a number of the Trappist beers (Chimay, Rochefort, Achel, Westmalle), strong blondes (like Duvel, La Chouffe), and abbey beer (Leffe, Maredsous, St. Feuillien).

However, if you'd like something particularly special, or you just

152

want some good advice, these are Andrew's top beer stores in Brussels:

Délices & Caprices is conveniently located just around the corner from Grand Place, on Rue des Bouchers (one of the only good reasons to venture to this street). Delices & Caprices has about 200 different beer available, and the owner, Pierre Zuber, is a friendly sort, originating from Switzerland. If you visit, you can enjoy a beer before you buy or even book a tasting session. Rue des Bouchers, 68

Beer Mania is near the European Parliament, on Chaussée de Wavre, just off of Rue du Trône. Again, the owner, Nasser Eftekhari, is passionate about the different types of beer available and is easy to chat with. There is also a small tasting area and a larger area upstairs where they host events, such as jazz nights. 174-176 Chausse de Wavre

Malting Pot, a relative new-comer on the beer scene, in Brussels, is just up from Place Flagey, on Rue Scarron. They focus on artisanal, craft beer and have a selection from around the world, not just Belgium. Shop owner, Sam Sarmad, knows his beer and can provide some really good selections: the Vivien Porter he recommended was stellar! Rue Scarron 50

Mig's World Wines

It's easy to find European wines in Brussels. In fact, any decent-sized grocery store will have a good selection. But if you're looking for a great 'new world' wine or something from a lesser known wine region, there's only one shop to visit – **Mig's World Wines**. Created by Miguel, aka Mig, a Belgian raised in Australia (hence the kangaroo on the logo) Mig's is a treasure trove of undiscovered wines. If you can't find something unique and tasty from Mig's stock of over 700 wines, he'll do his utmost to find what you're looking for and order it for you.

Mig's also carries a variety of Belgian beer and speciality spirits, like whiskeys, tequilas and liqueurs. If you're looking for a special alcoholic treat from Belgium, Mig's is your one stop shop. You'll be surprised at the variety of spirits and wine created within Belgium's tiny borders. Mig's is one of the few places in Brussels you can purchase the excellent Belgian sparkling wine (to rival any Champagne) from Domaine des Agaises. The friendly and helpful staff of Mig's are always ready to help you find the perfect bottle from any corner of the globe. Mig's World Wines - Chaussée de Charleroi 43

Chai & Bar

Chai & Bar perfectly combines two of my favourite things—wine and food. This wine shop, in Uccle, claims a prime spot on the Chaussée de Waterloo. The store stocks roughly 900 different wines, from around the world, but primarily focusing on Europe. Their Bordeaux selection is unparalleled, with over 400 varieties.

But the best part of Chai & Bar is the unique tasting bar, where you can sample 8 to 16 different wines from their current stock. These can be pared with a charcuterie and cheese selection for the ultimate tasting experience. The friendly staff is always happy to help you choose the perfect bottle to match any meal. Chai & Bar - Chaussée de Waterloo 1469

HOTELS FOR FOODIES

There are hundreds of hotels in Brussels and many excellent options to suit all styles and budgets. The hotels I've listed in this guide have been chosen specifically with foodies in mind. These hotels either have great restaurants themselves, or are in close proximity to some of the city's best restaurants.

These particular hotels tend to be on the higher end of the budget spectrum. Most of my favourite budget hotels in Brussels don't have their own restaurant and/or are situated farther from the city centre and the better dining options. However, if budget is a concern, and you don't mind staying outside of the city, visit my website for more (non-foodie) hotel options.

The Hotel

If money is no object, **The Hotel** is my 'must stay' hotel in Brussels. After all, how can you go wrong staying at place called THE Hotel?

This ultra-modern mega-hotel is just steps from the exclusive shopping of Brussels' Avenue Louise and Boulevard de Waterloo. Spacious rooms start at 25m² (247 ft²) and get larger, as your price increases, of course. The rooms tick all of my boxes for attention to detail, including King-sized beds, Nespresso machines for your morning coffee fix, free unlimited wifi, bright reading lights, beautiful design, nice toiletries, complementary water, and the best shower-head I've had in all of Europe.

However, the best in-room feature is the long sofa beneath the expansive windows, so you can make the most of your view - and what a view it is. From the upper floors, you can admire the entire Brussels skyline.

Beyond the great room, The Hotel has some additional perks. The Panorama Lounge (for the exclusive use of guests staying in the Deluxe Panorama rooms) offers free-flowing Belgian beer, wine, champagne, and organic fruit juices. There is also a selection of delicious desserts.

The Urban Spa is small, but the sauna has a glass wall offering a stunning view of the Brussels skyline. What a way to unwind!

Especially for foodies, the gastronomic restaurant, **The Restaurant**, is a must. Head chef, Pierre Balthazar, invited three international guest chefs, to help compose a menu that is a world tour, based on 9 key ingredients. This is **not** your typical hotel food.

The Bar is one of my favourite places for cocktails in Brussels (See the Drinks section above) and their afternoon tea and cakes are a delight.

If you want a hotel that is so much more than just a place to lay your head at night, The Hotel should be your top pick. The Hotel - Boulevard de Waterloo 38 (Read my extended review of The Hotel and The Restaurant)

Radisson Blu Royal

For central location, luxury, and great food, you'd be hard pressed to top the **Radisson Blu Royal Hotel**, just steps from Grand Place. It's home to Brussels' 2-star Michelin restaurant, Sea Grill (see The Stars above) and the Ginotheque (see the Drinks section) for creative cocktails.

The Standard and Business Class rooms are spacious (26m^2) and include free wifi, coffee and tea service, air conditioning, a safe, and flat screen TVs. Business class will also give you access to the Fitness Club and include the giant buffet breakfast. For even more opulence, the Executive Suites are vast and contain everything you need for a luxurious home-away-from-home.

If Sea Grill is beyond your budget, the Radisson's **Atrium restaurant** is a great alternative. Less formal, but still elegant, the dining room is in the huge open atrium of the hotel and features a section of the old Brussels city wall.

The menu ranges from seasonal dishes to traditional favourites, with items like: a duo of smoked quail breast and seared foie gras with a cream of sweet potatoes; and oven-roasted 'Piétrain' pork filet and crawfish tails.

In addition, the Radisson Blu Royal is steps from Brussels' top sights like Grand Place, the museums of Mont des Arts, and Place Sainte Catherine, not to mention countless great restaurants and shops for foodies. Radisson Blu Royal Hotel - Rue du Fosse-aux-Loups 47 (Read my extended review of the Radisson Blu Royal Hotel and Atrium Restaurant)

The Dominican

The Dominican Hotel, in central Brussels, takes its name from its location on the site of a former Dominican abbey. It's now a luxurious hotel with an interior that contrasts its classical architecture with modern design. Rooms are tranquil, plush, and comfortable, and the hotel is entirely non-smoking.

You can dine in the beautiful Grand Lounge or enjoy the outdoor Court Yard Bistro on a sunny summer's day. The trendy black and orange Lounge Bar is a Brussels favourite nightspot. Open until at least 1am, the cocktails are popular with the city's 'in-crowd' as well as hotel guests. It's also located close to Grand Place and many of Brussels' top restaurants, including the nearby Belga Queen. The Dominican Hotel - Rue Léopold 9

Thon Hotel EU

For an ethical hotel choice in Brussels that is also beautiful, modern, comfortable, and perfectly located for business and pleasure, look no farther than the **Thon Hotel EU**.

The Thon Hotel EU is a Green Key certified property, meaning it meets high standards for environmental and social sustainability. So along with comfort and design – you get a guilt-free night's sleep.

In addition to addressing concerns about waste, water and energy management; green open spaces; food; environmental education; and mobility, the hotel also focuses on environmental innovation. They keep beehives on their green roof and use the honey in the restaurant. The breakfast buffet is vast and includes some local and organic products. They even have their own organic Belgian beer available in the bar.

The hotel also offers guests free Villo bike rental passes. If guests opt not to have their room serviced, they receive a 5 euro voucher that can be used throughout the hotel or donated to Good Planet, which teaches young people about environmental responsibility and sustainability issues.

In addition to locally sourced ingredients and their organic beer, the Thon EU is a short walk or metro ride to central Brussels' restaurants or head to Place Jourdan for fewer tourists and Brussels' best *frites* at Maison Antoine. Thon Hotel EU - Rue de la Loi/Wetstraat 75 (Read my extended review of the Thon Hotel EU)

Hotel Bloom

Hotel Bloom is an excellent choice if you love art and design as much as food. It's also easier on the wallet than many of the city's other hotel/restaurant combos.

On the design side, Hotel Bloom offers plenty of character and bold colours. Each room is designed by a different European art student, featuring a unique piece of art, created especially for the hotel. This individuality carries into the restaurant where different seating areas create different moods - hence the restaurant name - **Smoods**.

In all honesty, I've had a hit and miss relationship with Smoods. As the menu changes seasonally, I've had some excellent dining experiences (a fall game menu springs to mind) and some that were less than remarkable.

The newest addition to Hotel Bloom is the **OO! Breakfast bar**, featuring its own Belgian waffle truck, for bake-your-own waffles.

With its fun and colourful vibe, and location close to the centre, and next to the Botanique exhibition space and botanical gardens, Hotel Bloom offers excellent affordable accommodation, in Brussels. Hotel Bloom - Rue Royal 250

MY PERFECT FOODIE DAY IN BRUSSELS

I'm often asked how to spend a foodie day in Brussels. Of course, everyone's taste and priorities are different. The perfect day depends on the season, the weather, and the company. But if I had one gloriously sunny day in Brussels, this is what I would do.

If I'm honest, I'd love to sleep in on my perfect day, but as today is all about food, the first thing I'm going to do is pop down to my local street market, in St. Josse. This isn't a particularly remarkable market; it's much the same as the markets that take place all over the city. We have one excellent Dutch fishmonger, a jolly Italian who sells cheese and fresh pasta, a German baker (Andrew loves his dense German loaves), and a lovely lady from Wallonia who makes the best pâtés and boudin I've ever tasted. Our market takes place every Thursday, but Brussels has street markets every day of the week, in different neighbourhoods.

10:00 am - Once I drop off my fresh market goodies at home, I'm going to head through Park Royal, down Mont des Arts, to **Aksum Coffee House** for the perfect coffee to start my day. I'm not a breakfast eater, but I need my morning caffeine to get me moving.

10:45 am - Caffeinated and ready to roll, it's time to do some foodie shopping. My first stop, on the way to the Sainte Catherine area is

Pappabubble. Here I pick up a couple of bags of my favourite hard candy (likely mojito and spicy cinnamon).

11:00 am - As I haven't had breakfast (and there are no calories on my perfect day) my next stop is for a duo of grey shrimp croquettes from the counter of **Zoordzee/Mer du Nord**. As the fish-bar is just opening, I won't have to wait in line. The croquettes are molten hot from the fryer and just the pick-me-up I need.

11:30 am - My next stop is across the street at **Champigros** for some foie gras from Southwest France. I'll peruse the fresh mushrooms too, to see what's in season.

11:45 am - Next I'll take a quick peek in **Frederic Blondeel** and see what's on offer for delicious chocolates. I may also register for an upcoming workshop.

12:00 pm - Now it's time to wander into **Kam-Yuen,** to stock up on all my Asian supplies. I never know exactly what I'm going to find here, but I always leave with something I didn't count on. The pretty Chinese pottery in the back corner, always draws my gaze, and the frozen dumplings are almost irresistible.

1:00 pm - All of this shopping has made me hungry, so I head to **Samourai Ramen** for a big bowl of noodle soup. Looking at the dumplings at Kam-Yuen inspires my decision to order gyoza, as well (not that I need further inspiration to eat dumplings.) I'll wash it all down with a mug of green tea.

2:00 pm - Now it's time to walk back up hill, so it's a good thing I've fuelled up. On the way, I'll stop at the **International House of Cooking**, to see if there are any new kitchen gadgets I can't live without. I'll also see what's new in the cookbook room.

3:00 pm - No day in Brussels is perfect without chocolate, so my next stop is **Grand Sablon**. I'll pop into the **Dandoy** biscuit shop for a box of speculoos, before making the rounds of my favourite chocolatiers. I'll be sure to look at the window display, of **Pierre Marcolini**, to see what new and innovative flavour combination is on offer this month. Then I'll go inside and buy a few of my favourites: café cardamom, caramel fondant, mango, ginger, and my favourite coeur framboise (raspberry heart) are sure to be in the box.

4:00 pm - It's time for a bit of a rest after all the retail therapy, so I head upstairs at **Wittamer**, to the Tea Room, and order their decadent hot chocolate. If you haven't had a hot chocolate in Belgium, you haven't had hot chocolate. This is thick, rich, and nothing but dark chocolate and cream. Heavenly. Of course, it comes with a little cookie and a few chocolates for good measure.

4:30 pm - Because I don't want to take my purchases to dinner, I'm going to pop home and freshen up. (You can head to your hotel if you're following my footsteps.) Luckily, Brussels' public transportation is cheap and efficient (no matter how much we locals like to complain about it.) It's also a bit before rush hour, so it's a good time to head out.

7:00 pm - Bruxellois like to eat later in the evening so, I'm going to head to **Le Wine Bar**, for a big glass of red wine, before supper. I don't want to spoil my dinner, especially after all the snacks I've had today, but I know Andrew will order the charcuterie plate. (You didn't think I'd eat alone on my perfect day did you?) We'll chat with the owner about his delicious cured meats. We could just stay here for dinner; I would inevitably order the *Joue de bœuf de l'Aubrac braisée au vin rouge* (Aubrac beef cheek in red wine). However, tonight we have reservations at a nearby favourite.

8:00 pm - Arriving at **L'Idiot du Village** we are warmly ushered through the quirky dining room to our reserved seat. (Reservations are an absolute must here.) We start with an apero of a kir royal (champagne and cassis), while we contemplate the menu. The specials are always tempting so we'll probably just let the server persuade us. Good dinners in Brussels are a long, lingering affair, filled with wine, conversation, and excellent food.

11:30pm - On my perfect day, I have more stamina than usual, and opt for an after dinner drink at The Bar. **The Bar** manager, Fabrizio, is on duty tonight and he makes the world's best dirty martini. He'll mix anything you like, but he's particularly great at choosing the perfect cocktail for you. We're in excellent hands, after a perfect foodie day in the world's best, undiscovered, foodie city.

MENU WORDS DICTONARY

Belgians (like their French neighbours to the south) **love** complex menu descriptions. This can make ordering a minefield, if you aren't familiar with French or Dutch. Increasingly, restaurants are using English in their menus, to cater to the large international community in Brussels, however, many still only print their *cartes* in the local languages. Below, I've listed a few food words, in both languages, to make your menu selection easier.

English	French	Dutch
Starter	une entrée	voorgerecht
Main Course	plat principal (or simply plat)	hoofdgerecht
Dessert	le dessert	dessert
Chicken	Poulet or volaille (fowl)	Kip
Meat (usually beef)	La viande (meat) Le bifteck (Steak)	Vlees (meat) Rund (beef)
Pork	Le porc	varken
Fish	Le poisson	vis
Vegetarian	Végétarien	Vegetarisch (food) vegetariër (person)
Cheese	Le fromage	kaas
Bread	Le pain	brood

Pasta	Les pâtes	pasta
Beer	La bière	pintje
Wine red/white/pink	Vin blanc/rouge/rosé	Wijn witte/rode/rose
Coffee	Le café	koffie
Tea	Thé	thee
Roasted	Rôti	geroosterd
Steamed	À la vapeur	gestoomd
Stuffed	Farci	gevuld
Fried	Frit(e)	gebakken
The Menu	La Carte	Menu
The Bill/Check	L'addition	De rekening
Allergic to	Allérgique à	Allergisch voor
Breakfast	Le petit-déjeuner	ontbijt
Lunch	Le déjeuner	lunch
Dinner	Le dîner	avondmaal
Medium Rare	À point	medium
Well Done	Bien cuit	doorbakken
Rare	saignant	rare
Blue	Bleu	rauw

NOW WHAT?

Now it's your turn to uncover your favourite Brussels foodie secrets. With this guide, you have the insight and knowledge to eat like a local. You can avoid the tourist traps, use your time and money wisely, and maybe even splurge on a truly unforgettable foodie experience.

Thanks for joining me on this food-filled adventure through Europe's undiscovered foodie Mecca. If you've enjoyed it as much as I've enjoyed sharing my secrets with you, please take a moment to share your opinion with other readers on Amazon. Reviews are vital to an indie-author's success and I appreciate every single one.

Don't forget to grab your free resources included with this book, by visiting http://cheeseweb.eu/fgb:

- A detailed Google Map of all locations listed in this guide
- The Top 10 Things to Do in Belgium ebook
- Our Favourite Food Blogs for Brussels
- Sneak-peeks and updates on all of our upcoming guides to Belgium and beyond

I wish you many fabulous foodie adventures in Brussels and beyond... Bon Appetit!

ABOUT THE AUTHOR

Alison Cornford-Matheson is a freelance writer and travel photographer whose work has appeared in AFAR, Outside, and Wanderlust magazines. Alison landed in Belgium in 2005, where she founded CheeseWeb.eu, a guide for expats and travellers dedicated to slow travel in Europe and beyond; including eating, shopping, exploring, and living the good life.

In May of 2015, Alison and her husband, Andrew, left Belgium to embark on their full-time, slow travel adventure. They are currently driving throughout Europe in their motorhome, Amelia, with their two cats, Buddy and Orange. You can follow their travels on CamperCats.com.

Alison is a founding member of the Professional Travel Bloggers Association. She contributes to luxury travel website Jetsetter, and is an Ambassador and Local Expert for AFAR.com.

She is a passionate traveller and loves to uncover 'hidden gems,' be they museums, shops, restaurants, castles, gardens or landscapes, and share them through her words and photos. She is also a foodie, music fan, garden enthusiast, and lover of all furry creatures. You can see all of these topics reflected in her work.